Supporting Young People Coping with Grief, Loss and Death

A Lucky Duck Book

Contents

Psychological Effects of Loss and Bereavement 1

Death 4

Emotional Literacy and Mental Health 6

How to Use the Programme – Notes for Facilitators 7

Session 1: Understanding Loss 13

Session 2: Divorce and Separation 19

Session 3: Belonging 27

Session 4: A Matter of Life and Death 39

Session 5: Facts and Figures 47

Session 6: Beliefs and Customs 63

Session 7: Feelings and Thoughts 91

Session 8: Questions and Answers 97

Session 9: The Grief Cycle 105

Session 10: Support and Communication 113

Session 11: Remembering and Celebrating 123

Session 12: Review 129

References 133

How to use the CD-ROM

The CD-ROM contains PDF files, labelled 'Worksheets.pdf' which consists of worksheets for each lesson in this resource. You will need Acrobat Reader version 3 or higher to view and print these resources.

To photocopy the worksheets directly from this book, align the edge of the page to be copied against the leading edge of the copier glass (usually indicated by an arrow).

Psychological Effects of Loss and Bereavement

When children or adults experience a significant loss, separation or bereavement they grieve. Grieving helps us to adapt to change and move on with our lives. If we do not grieve, we run the risk of carrying unresolved emotional issues into other parts of our lives. In order to understand loss, separation and bereavement and the process of grief, it is necessary to understand how we form attachments and how our emotional wellbeing is dependent on the quality of our significant relationships.

Bowlby's attachment theory

Bowlby's attachment theory is based on the notion that humans are driven to connect to others, and that as babies we are 'programmed' to bond emotionally with our 'primary care-giver(s)'. These are usually our parents. This bond is made through ordinary parenting behaviour which includes being fed, nurtured, held, protected and communicated with. These primary attachments allow us to survive. They also provide the foundation for our longer term mental health and ability to form relationships.

If a primary attachment is strong, the child will feel confident, secure and loved. Once established, a child will be able to make a healthy separation from the primary caregiver and will relate well to other people, i.e. they will themselves make healthy attachments.

If a primary attachment is insecure a child will become anxious and feel insecure. Difficulties may arise both when separating from the primary caregiver and in developing trusting relationships.

When a primary attachment is broken (by bereavement or other means) during early childhood, the pain of the loss can literally feel 'life-threatening'. The child will be in terrible emotional pain which may express itself physically. A period of mourning and grieving will be necessary and recovery may only be partial. The loss will literally shape the child's psychological development.

There is now consensus that many mental health problems presented by adults often stem from unresolved childhood losses and the breaking of these primary attachment bonds. (Black 1978, Bowlby 1979).

The biochemistry of attachment and loss

Bowlby's theories are both confirmed and clarified by current developments in our understanding of the brain, which shows that there is a biochemical dimension to attachment and loss.

Primary attachments are rooted in brain and body chemistry (Sunderland M. 2003). When we are intimate, loving and playful, natural opioid like chemicals in the brain and hormones in the body are released. These are drug-like in the way they motivate us to want to be with the person who makes us feel like this. Even thinking about and remembering people with whom we have a primary attachment has a biochemical dimension.

When we lose someone to whom we are deeply attached we experience a withdrawal from these positive brain states. Our anxiety level may rise, as will the levels of stress hormones in our bodies, and we may feel depressed. Depending on circumstances, this change in biochemistry can also generate the release of chemicals which make us feel angry or hostile.

As Sunderland states, in the light of these biochemical facts it is not surprising to learn that:

'Seventy per cent of men in prison suffered a broken attachment in childhood,'(NACRO).

'The biggest group of children who are excluded from school for bad behaviour before the age of nine are the group who have suffered a bereavement,' (Home Office Statistics 2001).

(quoted in Sunderland 2003)

Similarly:

…'parental bereavement may put an individual at greater risk of social exclusion and mental health difficulties,' (Ribbens McCarthy, 2005, p68).

Encouragingly, it seems that biochemical distress can be reduced through being comforted and by being encouraged to stay calm. When a child who experiences a major loss is comforted, natural brain opioids will be released. Remaining calm allows biochemical distress to subside. It is therefore vital that children who experience a major loss are both physically comforted and enabled to remain in a calm state.

While our capacity for strong primary attachment is at its greatest, and is indeed essential in infancy, we now know that strong attachments can be made at any point in our lives. For example, when we fall in love and when we become parents the same chemicals and hormones help us to form new attachments.

Positive warm relationships at any age can therefore help build a healthy brain and improve our emotional wellbeing – literally, our mental health.

Thus it is that when a child, or adult, is grieving, it will be contact with and connection to caring people that will provide both comfort and the potential for recovery. Additionally, the chance to remember the person, and to talk about them, will be useful in terms of being able to make a healthy 'separation' and 'move on'.

Loss

There are many different types of loss and a wide variation in the ways in which individuals experience and respond to loss. Feelings of loss will be experienced in a bereavement but also in relation to events such as the birth of a sibling, divorce, moving house, losing a toy and so on. It is important for adults to recognise that even small losses for children and adolescents can become quite significant and can also impact on how they later respond to bigger or more significant losses.

For children and younger adolescents the experience of loss can be quite different to that of an adult. This is because they have less experience on which to draw when making sense of what has happened to them. They are more likely to feel overwhelmed by their feelings. Also, because children have less control over their circumstances and environment they are generally dependent on the adults around them to notice when they are grieving a loss.

A wide range of behaviours or responses to loss have been identified, as follows:

Cognitive
- regression to previous level of skills
- loss of skills
- reluctance to communicate
- difficulties in communicating
- confusion over what has happened
- difficulties in sequencing (order and time)
- being unable to make up your mind about things
- inability to concentrate or attend
- loss of memory
- decrease in reasoning skills
- decrease in academic output/functioning.

Supporting Young People Coping with Grief, Loss and Death

Deborah Weymont & Tina Rae

Paul Chapman Publishing

© Deborah Weymont and Tina Rae 2006

First published 2006

Apart from any fair dealing for the purposes of research or private study, or criticism or review, as permitted under the Copyright, Designs and Patents Act 1988, this publication may be reproduced, stored or transmitted in any form, or by any means, only with the prior permission in writing of the publishers, or in the case of reprographic reproduction, in accordance with the terms of licences issued by the Copyright Licensing Agency. Enquiries concerning reproduction outside those terms should be sent to the publishers.

Rights to copy pages marked as handouts, certificates or overhead foils are extended to the purchaser of the publication for his/her use.

The right of the author to be identified as Author of this work has been asserted by him/her in accordance with the Copyright, Design and Patents Act 1988.

Paul Chapman Publishing

A SAGE Publications Company

1 Oliver's Yard

55 City Road

London EC1Y 1SP

SAGE Publications Inc.

2455 Teller Road

Thousand Oaks, California 91320

SAGE Publications India Pvt Ltd.

B-42, Panchsheel Enclave

Post Box 4109

New Delhi 110 017

www.luckyduck.co.uk

Commissioning Editor: Barbara Maines

Editorial Team: Mel Maines, Sarah Lynch, Wendy Ogden

Designer: Jess Wright

Illustrations by: Deborah Weymont and Mark Ruffle

A catalogue record for this book is available from the British Library

Library of Congress Control Number 2005907010

ISBN10 1-4129-1311-X   ISBN13 978-1-4129-1311-9

ISBN10 1-4129-1312-8 (pbk)   ISBN13 978-4129-1312-6 (pbk)

Printed on paper from sustainable resources

Printed in Great Britain by The Cromwell Press Ltd, Trowbridge, Wiltshire

Psychological
- obsessional behaviours
- loss of concentration
- loss of attention
- personality changes
- increase in nightmares or scary dreams
- fear that the event will recur
- concerns for others within the family or social context.

Emotional
- the need to be looked after by others
- feelings of sadness
- feelings of depression and anxiety
- guilt, anger and shame
- mood swings
- concerns and worries about losing someone else or something else that is valuable and important to the individual.

Behavioural
- clinging behaviours
- regression to more babyish behaviours
- obsessive and repetitive talking
- aggression and disobedience
- decrease in ability to self control or discipline
- abuse of alcohol or drugs
- reluctance to attend school
- withdrawal
- being disorganised
- feeling and being distant from others
- feeling or being unpredictable or irritable
- physical symptoms
- lying or stealing.

Physical
- experiencing headaches
- experiencing stomachaches
- experiencing shock
- experiencing constriction of the throat
- disturbed sleep
- feeling tired and listless
- loss of appetite
- loss of control physically
- avoidance of others and social contexts
- unable to cope with established and regular routines (home and school).

Death

Every day about forty children under sixteen will lose a parent through death (Wells R 1998). There are also many others who are bereaved through the death of someone they love such as a grandparent, a sibling, another relative, friend or trusted adult. Although exact figures are unclear, the majority (and possibly as many as 92%) of under 16's in this country report having experienced a significant bereavement (Ribbens McCarthy 2005).

While the prevalence and effects of divorce and separation on young people have been widely researched (Rogers, B. & Pryor, J. 1998) there is little accurate information about the impact of bereavement.

The information we do have raises important questions:

'...from the possible implications of parental death for long-term risk of depression, to the frequency of experiences of bereavement among young offenders,' (Ribbens McCarthy 2005 p1).

While bereavement is not always or necessarily linked to negative outcomes when taken alongside other factors relating to individual vulnerability, family circumstances and social disadvantage, it is identified as a significant 'risk factor' in young people's lives.

'...bereavement may carry implications for educational and learning processes and outcomes, for early home leaving, for early sexual activities and poor health behaviours, and possibly for aggressive or delinquent behaviours.'(ibid p40)

In terms of implications for policy and practice, Ribbens McCarthy (2005) draws a number of conclusions about these links. This includes a call for better integrated services, targeting of resources and the need for more research alongside ensuring young people's views are included. Additionally, and of particular relevance to the task of this programme, she is unequivocal about the need to include death education in the school curriculum:

'Death education needs to be much more widely and systematically included in schools, as a key aspect of general education for life, and as a way of equipping individuals to help both themselves and others through mutual support and understanding in relation to bereavement experiences,' Ibid p69.

Children's understanding of death

Previously, it was believed that children didn't or couldn't grieve because they had an immature concept of death. However, current thinking shows that while children do perceive death differently to adults, they do grieve, but in their own way. Children will tend to understand and react to death according to their age and developmental level. Their understanding and reactions are also linked to the manner in which the person has actually died. For example, a child's response to a sudden traumatic bereavement will be different from a death following a long illness.

The developmental stages for children's understanding of death (Pennels, M. & Smith, S.C., 1995, Pettlle, S.A. & Britten, C.M. 1995) are as follows:

Age 0 - 2

The bereaved child will usually seek the presence of the person who died. They will experience a sense of loss but will not be able to put it into words or understand that this loss is permanent.

Age 2 - 4

Children under the age of five have an idea that death exists. They do not, however, understand that it is final and they may continually question others as to when the dead person is going to return to them.

Age 5 - 9

At this stage children can begin to understand irreversibility. However, they often have a greater sense and awareness of feelings of guilt and they may feel to some extent responsible for the death. Children may personalise death as some form of monster and may show some curiosity around the rituals surrounding death and funerals. At this stage children can often deny their own grief when they feel that this will protect an adult's feelings, e.g. the remaining parent.

Age 9 -12

At this age, children have a more adult understanding of the finality of death and of their own mortality. While some children may experience great anxiety when bereaved, other children may deny feeling any sense of loss or bereavement and simply try to continue with life as normal i.e. remaining in denial.

Adolescents

Adolescents tend to grieve in a similar way to adults. However, their emotions tend to be less contained and they may be less able to process the powerful emotions associated with bereavement. A bereavement may add urgency to their questions about the meaning of life and can further prompt suicidal thoughts and feelings.

Loss and death education for adolescents

This book has been devised primarily for use with adolescents, whom we believe to be particularly vulnerable in relation to experiences of loss and death. They also tend to be receptive to exploring these sorts of issues.

The programme explores loss in its widest sense and includes the experience of divorce and separation and loss, such as being placed in care or of being a refugee, as well as death. These more complex losses are often not acknowledged in a school context, but in fact they involve significant changes which may need to be mourned. Also, adolescents are typically in the process of separating from their families and often feel 'alone' and 'outside'. A family bereavement can force them to assume a more adult role than they are ready for. A major loss or bereavement can exaggerate the ordinary process of mourning the loss of childhood, and may increase their sense of isolation. Helping adolescents understand either their own experiences or those of others can both put things in perspective and improve emotional literacy.

By encouraging students to talk about loss and death and their feelings we normalise loss, bereavement and change. We externalise what is usually internalised. We also challenge the taboo that surrounds talking about death openly in our culture, and we gain a healthier perspective on both our own losses and those of others.

We think teachers, psychologists and support staff in schools have a key role to play in developing a healthier attitude to death. As Barbara Ward & Associates state in their book *Good Grief* (1993):

'If we don't mourn losses at the time they happen, major problems, e.g. severe depression, can be triggered when later losses occur.'

Again, the fact that one in five children will now be affected by divorce further underlines the urgency of educating children about loss.

We think it is vital that the emotional needs of children who have experienced major loss and who are bereaved are both acknowledged and to an extent, met within schools. Not only will the school become a happier, more emotionally literate place, in which to learn and work; there will be longer-term preventative effects relating to social inclusion and mental health.The known links between childhood bereavement, behavioural difficulties, school exclusion and later psychological problems make it imperative that we develop effective preventative interventions. Schools are well-placed to play a key role in this (Ribbens McCarthy, 2005).

Emotional Literacy and Mental Health

There is a growing demand for resources and materials to support the development of children's emotional literacy. Emotional literacy is seen to both address wider issues of social inclusion alongside helping individuals to learn and develop positive relationships. Sharp (2001) gives four reasons for promoting emotional literacy. He suggests that human beings need to:

1. recognise their emotions in order to be able to label or define them
2. understand their emotions in order to become effective learners
3. handle or manage their emotions in order to develop sustained positive relationships
4. appropriately express emotions in order to develop as 'rounded people' who are able to help themselves and, in turn, those around them.

McCarthy and Park (1998) say that there are strong links between emotional literacy, cognitive development and mental heath. They make the following points:

- Understanding emotions is directly connected to both cognitive achievements and motivation to learn.
- Dealing effectively with emotions helps individuals to develop more positive relationships and provides a sense of mental or psychological wellbeing.
- Those adolescents who are 'emotionally developed' are deemed to be better able to live with or cope with difference.
- Moral views and value systems are shaped by both attitudes and feelings.
- The sense of purpose and meaning that individuals gain in their lives is derived in equal parts from both feelings and understanding.

This sort of research has generated much interest and many initiatives in education. The most comprehensive of these has been in the DfES Primary National Strategy pilot of the social, emotional and behavioural skills (SEBS) curriculum, which is now being introduced throughout KS1 and KS2.

While this does include some work on grief with younger children, little attention has been paid to working with older children or the broader themes of loss and death education which this programme addresses.

We believe that children and young adults need to have acknowledged both the small and more significant losses that they experience in their lives and that adults in both the home and school context need to deal with loss and death more openly. This programme has therefore been developed to better equip both teachers and students with the knowledge, skills and attitudes necessary to manage loss and death more effectively in all our lives.

Traumatic loss

Teachers should note that while the programme explores some aspects of traumatic loss it is not intended to target children who have personal experience of traumatic loss and bereavement. Typically these children will exhibit many of the behaviours on pages 2 and 3, with great intensity and over a long period of time. It is likely that therapy will be more suitable for such children.

We strongly recommend that you use the facilitator's checklist as a way of preparing yourself to run this programme and help identify children for whom the content of this programme may be inappropriate. While you are probably already aware of those pupils who find it difficult to learn in a classroom setting, the checklist will help you focus more specifically on identifying pupils who may be particularly vulnerable in relation to the content of this programme and differentiate accordingly.

Please note: The programme similarly does not specifically address the issue of the death of a pupil or a member of staff. There are some resources available on the DfES website (www.teacher.net.gov.uk) and further resources and information can be obtained from useful websites listed at the end of this section.

How to Use the Programme – Notes for Facilitators

Planning

PSHE and Citizenship

This programme is designed to be delivered to groups or whole classes of secondary school students, either through extended tutor times or via the PSHE or Citizenship curriculum. The programme fulfils the requirements of the PSHE and Citizenship national curriculum in England as detailed in the document *Curriculum 2000*, Section 3: 'Developing good relationships and respecting differences between people'. Here it states that children should be taught about, 'the impact of separation, divorce and bereavement on families and how to adapt to changing circumstances.'

The programme is delivered in twelve sessions of between 45 and 90 minutes. However, both the programme and individual sessions can be used flexibly and should be tailored to suit context and to meet individual teachers' and students' requirements.

Use the facilitator's checklist

The facilitators checklist has been devised to both summarise and help staff focus on key issues that need to be addressed at the planning stage. This includes raising awareness of the needs of more vulnerable pupils, practical considerations relating to resources and wider policy implications within the school.

Facilitator notes are also provided in the Introduction to some sessions and for some activities where more explanatory detail is needed. These provide some hints and pointers as to when things may or may not require more sensitive handling.

A whole-school approach

It is hoped that this programme will further prompt facilitators to consider how effectively this kind of work is embedded in the curriculum and or how it can best be tailored to meet individual and whole-school needs. It may also prompt thinking as to how the school manages and supports those who are bereaved, similarly how the death of a pupil or member of staff is managed. A school which has an active policy and well-developed practice on emotional literacy is in a good position to respond creatively and appropriately to bereaved children.

Facilitator's checklist

Preparation for delivery of this programme must include both practical considerations relating to room use, resources and so on, as well as reflection on your own experience of loss, your skills as a facilitator and the need to reduce risk and create a learning environment which feels safe for the pupils.

This checklist has been developed to help facilitators prepare thoroughly. It may be useful as an exercise to help you establish priorities for discussion or action. It is not definitive and it may be appropriate to add other points that relate more specifically to your situation.

While it is not essential that you have all the knowledge, skills and experience implied below, it is essential that you are aware of your strengths and weaknesses and that you take the necessary steps to ensure you are well prepared.

Remember, loss and death education is an emotional topic and may arouse strong feelings and reactions. It is important that the facilitator feels able to 'hold' a group and is prepared to deal with difficulties that arise. It is also important that the learning process is itself 'emotionally literate' and that a supportive empathic and caring ethos is promoted from the start.

We recommend that two facilitators run the programme. This could be a 'lead facilitator' (e.g. a learning mentor or a teacher) supported by a learning support assistant. Having two facilitators means you can withdraw individuals if necessary. It also means one of you can take on an observer role if appropriate.

The lead facilitator should:

- have experience of delivering group work and Circle Time
- have a positive approach and proven skills in relation to social inclusion
- be committed to developing their own emotional literacy
- have a reflective approach to their teaching and learning
- understand how emotional literacy promotes mental health and school achievement.

Before starting this programme, facilitators should discuss any personal experience of loss with each other which may be helpful or unhelpful. Consideration should also be given to ways in which you will support each other during the programme.

If you are aware of a student who is currently experiencing loss or bereavement, talk to them separately before the sessions.

While it is possible to select individual activities, adapt sessions and structure the programme according to your situation and group, please note that the programme has been planned to be coherent and careful consideration has been given to the order in which themes have been introduced.

Whole-school readiness

- In your opinion, has the school dealt well with bereavements amongst staff and pupils?
- Does the school have an active policy on behaviour and bullying?
- Does the school have a member of staff responsible for SEN, travellers, homeless, looked after, adopted children and refugees?
- Are school exclusions dealt with systematically, fairly and as a last resort?
- Will you be supported by senior management?
- How will you deal with colleagues or parents/carers who have a strong negative reaction to this work?
- How will you explain the work to parents/carers?
- Is there a whole school policy on emotional literacy?
- To whom are you accountable in this role?

Reducing risk

- Think about writing a letter to parents and carers to either secure their consent or inform them of your intentions.
- Identify potentially vulnerable children prior to starting the group.

Do you feel confident to manage the contributions of:

- pupils at risk of exclusion?
- pupils underachieving?
- pupils who have been bereaved (recently or otherwise)?
- pupils who have experienced divorce and separation?

- pupils who have experienced the sorts of losses explored in Section 3. That is, pupils who are 'looked after', adopted or have refugee status.
- What self-management strategies will you use to prepare yourself for each session?
- Can you provide 1-1 time for pupils who need it? How will you identify those pupils?
- Will you evaluate each session on the same day it is held?
- How will 'lessons learned' when running this group, be fed into future planning for this work?
- When planning the programme, identify 'What if...?' worst case scenarios. This will help you anticipate and prevent problems.

Inclusion

- Is the classroom and the curriculum accessible to all learners? Will your lessons include everyone?
- How will you manage the introduction of differentiated tasks for some learners?
- How will you pay attention to different learning styles?
- Will your resources and anecdotes portray the world as exclusively young, white, middle-class, able-bodied and heterosexual?
- Will your displays represent the cultural diversity of our society? Will they challenge stereotypes?
- Will you challenge the discriminatory attitudes and practices of some pupils constructively?
- How are the needs of bi-lingual and ethnic minority learners met?
- What are your own beliefs about death, the afterlife and assisted death? How will you avoid bias?
- What are the dominant cultural values and/or religious beliefs in the school? In what ways will this help or hinder the effective delivery of the programme?

Group work and team-teaching

- Do you understand the difference between group work and working in groups?

Have you and your co-facilitator discussed:

- how much you will disclose
- how and when you will evaluate each session
- what happens if one of you is absent
- what you will do if a pupil is absent
- the benefits of having one of you taking an observer role for some activities
- a draft opening statement for your first session
- suggested ground rules
- how you will manage the paperwork?
- Do you have strategies for managing difficult individuals in groups? Do you have a shared view on how you will manage difficulties?
- Discuss how you would like to give each other feedback.

See also *Developing SEBS* Appendix 3 – Guidance on the teaching of potentially sensitive and controversial issues. DfES 2003.

Aims

When tailoring the programme the facilitator may want to use a selection from this list:

- to develop emotional literacy (that is, to recognise, understand, manage and express emotions in ourselves and others)
- to encourage students to become more aware of the links between feelings, thinking and behaviour
- to further develop their ability to reflect, joint problem-solve and work with others
- to develop empathy
- to increase self-esteem
- to develop confidence in dealing with difficult situations
- to improve students' social and group work skills
- to develop communication and relationship skills
- to promote resilience
- to help students identify and gain a deeper understanding of the feelings associated with loss, separation and bereavement
- to promote respect and tolerance
- to understand the grieving process and the ways in which people can be helped through this process
- to understand and value the afterlife beliefs, death rituals and funeral customs of other cultures and religions.

It would seem appropriate that these aims are used to help formulate the success criteria of the programme.

Preparation

Many of the resources, such as the photocopiable worksheets, the flip-chart and markers and the chairs set up in a circle for talk time can be organised prior to the start of the session. These are usually required in all twelve sessions.

Structure

The twelve sessions have been planned in this sequence:

Session 1: Understanding Loss

Session 2: Divorce and Separation

Session 3: Belonging

Session 4: A Matter of Life and Death

Session 5: Facts and Figures

Session 6: Beliefs and Customs

Session 7: Feelings and Thoughts

Session 8: Questions and Answers

Session 9: The Grief Cycle

Session 10: Support and Communication

Session 11: Remembering and Celebrating

Session 12: Review

Resources

Worksheets and facilitator's notes are provided as needed for each of the three activities in each session.

We recommend that you tailor your resources to suit your group. This could included altering our worksheets as well as finding source material, such as pop songs, video clips, poems, paintings, quotes from books and so on.

Record-keeping

The activity sheets can be presented in A4 folders or home-made project books in order to ensure that a special record is kept of each student's work. This can be used as a tool for self-reflection, encouraging the students to assess their own progress on the programme.

Delivery of each session follows the same structure:

Introduction

The introduction to the topic for each session is led by the facilitator and can include reference to the suggested illustration or quote. Alternatively, it may be more appropriate to use a topical item (e.g. in the news or from a TV soap).

The facilitator should also state the aims and planned outcomes for the session.

Talk time

Talk time activities are like ice-breakers. They can be used to get started and focused on the topic. They also set the scene with regard to student participation by promoting a sense of young people's views being valued and of interest. The intention is to foster a democratic teaching and learning environment in which discussion is welcomed and students are encouraged to generate solutions to their own problems. Talk time is group work based and will help students to develop key skills of working together, problem-solving and communication.

Activities

Each session has three suggested activities plus a number of follow-on activities. The activities are intended to develop knowledge, understanding and emotional literacy in relation to the focus of the session.

Most activities should be appropriate for mainstream KS3 and KS4 pupils. The third activity in each session is differentiated to meet the needs of less able and more reluctant pupils.

This programme is inclusive in the way each session contains activities that are suitable for mixed ability groups. The facilitator's skills at including less able pupils should be applied to further differentiate each activity as needed. This can include adapting worksheets as well as strategies, such as pairing less and more able pupils together.

Learning styles

The emphasis throughout the programme is on interpersonal and intrapersonal skills development (i.e. emotional literacy). Nonetheless, we think it is important that facilitators are aware of individual strengths and weaknesses and that they plan for the success of all children in their class. Consideration of different learning styles should prompt the facilitator to ensure a balanced range of visual, auditory and kinaesthetic based work, as well as activities that suit children with logical mathematical and or verbal linguistic strengths.

The activities may include completion of a worksheet or discussion based task. Sometimes the sheets may reinforce work covered in talk time. Some sheets can be completed independently whilst others require students to work as a pair or in a group.

Plenary

A brainstorm can be used to get students' views about each session and the relative usefulness of the work done. The plenary encourages students to reflect on the session, what they have learned and how they felt about the work.

This is an opportunity to recap and summarise the skills, concepts and ideas covered. It is also an opportunity for the facilitator to make conclusions, draw out the learning and remind students of the ground rules.

Follow-on activities

These are provided in order to reinforce key concepts and increase students' level of awareness and coping strategies.

The wide range of ideas for activities should make it possible to tailor a programme that is well suited to a particular group. It is unlikely that there will be time, or that it will be appropriate, to complete all the activities within each session.

Useful websites for resources and information

www.childbereavement.org.uk

www.crusebereavementcare.org.uk

www.stchristophers.org.uk

www.winstonswish.org.uk

Session 1
Understanding Loss

Introduction

The facilitator should start the session by briefly summarising both the content of the course and its aims. You may also want to say why loss and death education is important and why you think it should be included in the curriculum. It may be helpful to include some of the following points:

- Any kind of loss involves change. It means giving up a familiar state or way of life for something different and new. This is the basis for all grief.
- A pain of loss is something that can be physical, emotional or spiritual and everyone will experience loss at some point in our lives.
- If we don't mourn losses when they occur, this can lead to problems in the future.
- A loss or bereavement can effect our ability to concentrate and learn.
- This programme will help us to understand the experience of loss and death and the process of grieving.
- The programme will help us to talk about loss, death and bereavement and to develop an emotional vocabulary for doing this.
- The programme may also improve our ability to concentrate and learn and to maintain and develop positive relationships.
- One in five children in school will be affected by divorce and one in five will also be affected by mental health difficulties at some point in their lives.
- There is evidence to show that difficulties at school including school exclusions are linked with loss and bereavement.
- Loss and death are a normal part of life. Treating them as taboo subjects does not help us.

Warn the students that the course may be difficult, particularly for those who have had or are experiencing a loss or bereavement.

Remind the students of the systems of support that exist within the school.

Give permission for students to pass on certain activities if they don't feel able to participate.

Reassure students that their wishes, feelings and thoughts will be respected.

Please also refer to the facilitator's checklists.

Talk time

Ask the students to discuss the advantages and disadvantages of studying this topic.

Students can be placed in smaller groups so as to facilitate discussion and then feed back to the group as a whole.

The facilitator can highlight differences and similarities in the responses. The advantages of studying this subject will include some of what has been outlined in the introduction. Any concerns regarding perceived disadvantages should be picked up explicitly and addressed in Activity 1 where group rules will be set.

Activity 1 – Setting group rules

Setting group rules allows the facilitators and the students to establish a respectful and caring learning environment from the start. It is vital that students have the opportunity to contribute to this process in order to ensure proper ownership of what is discussed and then agreed.

Sometimes it can be useful if the facilitator has a prepared list of suggestions. For other groups the process of setting their own ground rules from their own baseline may be more useful. If possible, formulate positive statements, i.e. a list of 'dos' as opposed to a list of 'don'ts'. The following suggestions may be useful:

- We will listen to each other and respect each other's views.
- We will encourage each other to speak up and will avoid put-downs.
- We will try to take turns to talk without interrupting.
- Each person will speak for themselves and not for others.
- We will try to show empathy for each other.
- We will all try to get on with each other and help each other.
- We will respect differences in our cultural backgrounds and religious beliefs and faith systems.
- We will recognise and value differences in each other.
- What's said in this room stays in the room.
- We can talk to others about what we've done in the group and about our feelings, but we do not talk about individuals in the group.
- Tears are fine – crying is natural when we think about sad things.
- It's OK to choose to opt out of an activity or discussion. It's not OK to stop other people working.

Once group rules have been agreed, the facilitator can type them and the students can have a copy for future reference. It may also be helpful to ask students to 'sign up' to the agreed rules as a concrete way of showing their commitment to the group and way of working.

Activity 2 – Brainstorm 'What is loss?'

In pairs or small groups ask the students to discuss what loss is. They can pool their ideas together in order to make a list or brainstorm. Notes can be recorded on the worksheet 'What is loss?'. Students should be encouraged to think about the widest range of definitions and to share their ideas and experiences which may, of course, be very different. Students can consider their own losses alongside those that they have observed other people experiencing. These may include some of the following:

- Growing up.
- Starting school (separation from parents/carers).
- Changing school or nursery in order to enter primary or secondary school, i.e. transitions which can involve a loss of familiar surroundings, people, friends.
- Losing the attention of parents when a younger brother or sister is born into the family.
- The death of a brother or sister (which can result in parents being stressed and preoccupied and result in feelings of isolation and rejection).
- Parents changing jobs (the family may move to a new area and all family members having to give up friends and familiar places and contexts).
- A child feeling the loss of a mother who has returned to work after being at home.

- The loss of a parent through separation, divorce or death.
- The experience of loss by illness or ageing.
- Family or friends moving away and relationships ending.
- Families moving from one country to another and gaining refugee status, i.e. the loss of their own culture and way of life.
- Children being placed in care.
- Children being labelled as having some kind of special need which can result in a loss of self-esteem status, participation etc. This degree of loss clearly depends on the child's perception and how others perceive them as a result of this labelling process.
- Unemployment, redundancy or loss of job and the way in which this can lead to a loss of status, money, self-esteem.
- The loss of a home and the experience of homelessness.
- The loss of familiar surroundings when we have to go into hospital for an operation.
- The loss of innocence and self-esteem when a child is sexually abused.
- The losses experienced by those with serious illnesses such as cancer, AIDS or heart disease which can ultimately lead to death and involve the processes of harassment, rejection and isolation along the way.
- The losses encountered by those who misuse both legal and illegal drugs. This may include the loss of personality and a way of life and the contacts that go with this.
- The loss of a child through miscarriage or stillbirth.
- The losses experienced by those who cannot conceive a child.
- The loss of so-called 'normal' body image when surgery has to be undertaken, e.g. an amputation. This can lead to a grief-like reaction and clearly results in some form of trauma.
- The loss experienced by those whose vision and hearing goes in early or later life.
- The loss involved when people are labelled as being disabled in some way.
- School exclusion.
- Punishments and sanctions.

(Ward. B. et al (1993) pp17-19)

Students can feed back their ideas to the whole group. The facilitator can then make a few summary points. These may include:

- Losses can be small or great.
- Losses can be felt for a short time or over a long period.
- People experience loss in different ways.
- Loss affects us differently at different stages of our lives.
- How we manage major loss effects how we experience minor loss.

It may be useful as a group to discuss which of the losses appear to be the most significant and which the least significant and to discuss if this is a helpful thing to do or not.

Activity 3 – Feelings associated with loss

In order to better promote students' emotional literacy, it is useful to follow Activity 2 with an activity that which builds on that discussion but focuses on feelings.

In the whole group or smaller groups ask the students to brainstorm all the feelings they associate with loss.

Use the worksheet 'What Feelings Do We Associate With the Word Loss?' to make a written record of the brainstorm and to clarify the difference between thoughts and feelings. This activity will increase the awareness of the vocabulary that exists to describe the wide continuum of losses that we experience. It also reveals how the same feelings can be felt for different experiences.

Plenary

To review the learning that has taken place in the session, ask the students: 'What have we learnt about loss?' This can be done as a whole group discussion and recorded on a flip-chart.

This discussion is likely to mirror your introduction. Key points should include:

- Loss is something that touches all of us throughout our lives.
- There are many types of loss (big and little, temporary and permanent).
- Learning how to express the feelings associated with loss is important because if we avoid difficult and uncomfortable feelings, we may also be at risk of losing happy feelings as well.

Further closing remarks may also include:

- When we experience loss, what is most important is that our losses are acknowledged and that we have the opportunity to share with others how we feel and to be supported by them.
- The grieving process, although universal, is also a very individual experience. The intensity of the grieving process will depend on several variables – how people have experienced losses, personality traits, alongside their religious and cultural background and the kind of support available.
- Recovery from loss is possible. While we cannot 'wave a magic wand' and not have had the experience, we can try to understand it. Such experiences can be used as a process for moving onwards and growing.

Finally, the facilitator may like to invite the students to say what they would like to cover during the programme and if they have any questions about the programme. Do keep a record of this discussion and make sure you adapt the programme to include these requests.

Follow-on activities

Time-line – 'The ups and downs of life'

Ask students to record both losses and gains in their lives to date. This could be presented in a graph format or a pictorial life-story type chronology of significant events (e.g. starting school, moving house, the death of a pet and so on). Students could discuss these as a group activity.

It may be useful to highlight losses common to all of us and to then proceed to discuss ways in which the children felt supported or otherwise when experiencing some of the most significant losses. This will allow you to highlight current support systems available to students both in and out of school.

- Use the title 'Loss' as a prompt for a piece of creative writing.
- Students can consider and identify a piece of music which most represents for them feelings of loss. Students could play music to each other, describe how the music makes them feel and how it reflects a sense of loss that they may have experienced.
- Ask students to illustrate a poem or song that explores the theme of loss.

Understanding Loss

S1

What is loss?

Write a list of all the different types of loss you can think of:

1. ....

2. ....

3. ....

4. ....

5. ....

6. ....

7. ....

8. ....

9. ....

10. ....

What does the word loss mean? (Write your own definition.)

....

....

What Feelings Do You Associate with the Word 'Loss'?

Session 2
Divorce and Separation

Introduction

It will be useful to start this session with a recap of the ground rules agreed in the first session. You may want to have them typed and copies given to each pupil to place in their files.

The topic can be introduced by highlighting the fact that divorce and separation are two of the most significant forms of loss and that it will affect all of those involved in many different ways. You may want to add that divorce and separation can sometimes feel like a bereavement for both parents and children and each individual will need to grieve their loss in a way that suits them.

There will obviously be students within the group who have experienced both divorce and separation. As such the facilitator will need to be mindful of individual needs and coping strategies.

The facilitator may wish to use a poem, song or reading to open up the discussion to students through talk time. We suggest:

Wilson, J. (1992) Chapter 1 of *The Suitcase Kid*. Doubleday.

Pink (2001) *Family Portrait* – from the album *m!ssundaztood*.

Talk time

In pairs or small groups ask students to consider the following questions.

- What is a family?
- Is there such a thing as a 'perfect' family?

In the whole group get general feedback and then highlight any similarities or differences in the responses. You may want to add some summary comments such as:

- Family means lots of different things. It's about people we are connected to but it might be a social connection as well as, or instead of, a biological connection.
- Families can be small or big.
- There is no such thing as a perfect family. But there is a stereotype of normal family life and pressure from religion and the media to be perfect. So a lot of people feel like they have failed if their family isn't 'perfect'.

It may be helpful to highlight these facts:

- One in three marriages ends in divorce.
- One in three children are born outside of marriage.
- One in five will experience parental divorce by the age of 16 years.

Our notion of what a family is should take account of the statistics.

Many families are far removed from the stereotype of two parents with 2.4 children. You may also want to highlight the fact that families are very different in the 21st century to what they were in the time when the students' parents and grandparents grew up. It will also be necessary to consider cultural and ethnic differences and the way in which families can be 'nuclear', small or extended.

Overall, what is important is that we respect and acknowledge difference.

Activity 1 – Describe my family

Use the handout 'Joe's Family' as a prompt. Then invite students to write their own description of their family on the worksheet 'My Home and Family'..

This can be shared in groups and differences and similarities can be identified.

The facilitator can usefully summarise the activity by concluding:

- everyone has a birth mother and father
- everyone has important people in their lives
- a family is usually the people we have strong emotional connection to
- some of us live with our biological relatives, some of us don't
- children don't usually get to choose who they live with so sometimes your family is not exactly how you'd like it
- some of us live with a mix of biological relatives and people we are connected to for other reasons (step-relatives etc.)
- in some cultures and communities family 'blood-ties' are highly valued, in others friendship and shared beliefs are more important.

Activity 2 – How others feel

In this activity students are asked to consider a variety of people who have experienced a range of different types of loss related to family breakdown, as follows:

- A woman of 45 whose husband has just left her for a girl of 19.
- A child whose father has just left home in order to set up home with his new girlfriend.
- A mother whose partner has 'come out' as gay.
- A child whose best friend's parents have just split up.
- A child who has just found out his mother is having an affair.
- A child who has gone to live with his father whilst his sister has stayed with his mother.
- A child who has been put into foster care whilst her parents divorce.
- A father whose partner has taken all the children to live with her new partner and will not give him access without a fight.

These are provided as a photocopiable resource for you to make into cards. You may wish to add more to suit your group.

Divide the students into groups with a selection of cards (one for each person) to discuss. Ask the students to talk about their first reactions to this person. Ask them to think about the feelings. How would this person feel? What are other people going to feel? How are other people going to react?

It may be useful for someone to act as a scribe in order to summarise the feelings words used to describe each person's situation.

Activity 3 – Feeling connected

Give students the 'Feeling Connected' worksheet. They can then draw their own family trees and/or friendship ties and identify key members of the family with whom they are particularly close and with whom they would experience a real sense of loss should they lose them.

Plenary

The facilitator can encourage students to consider what they have learnt in this session about divorce and separation and the way in which people experience these kinds of losses. Students' views can be summarised on the flip-chart as key points. These may include the following:

- Families are diverse.
- Respecting difference in terms of how a family is now constituted is vital.
- It is also important to recognise the equality of people's feelings and experiences, e.g. feelings of loss experienced by a partner who has been left will not be any different to those experienced by a married partner who has just been left.

Follow-on activities

Role-play

The 'How Others Feel' cards can again be used for this activity which involves students working in pairs and role-playing each of the situations. One student can imagine that they are the person in question and can then be interviewed by their partner. It would be helpful for the partner to perhaps formulate a list of questions in order to structure the interview. These may include the following:

- Who are you?
- What's happened to you?
- What did other people do?
- How has this situation made you feel?
- How are you currently coping with the situation?
- What do you think might help you cope better in the future?

Students may wish to swap around at the end of the role-play so that both partners have an opportunity to be the character and the interviewer. The idea here is to reinforce the notion of empathy and the importance of being able to 'put yourself in someone else's shoes'. It is also important to encourage students to gain a further awareness of other people's lives and experiences and the way in which the processes of loss and grieving are common to all.

To come out of role-play properly, you may want to allow the students to re-establish their identities by saying, 'My name is... and I attend... school and I live at...

- Ask a member of Relate to come and talk to the group about the work of their organisation. Students could prepare questions in advance of this visit in order to make the most of the opportunity.
- Students can discuss what kinds of things would be helpful in terms of supporting children whose parents have split up or divorced. What can they themselves do? What can the school do to help? What can people in the community do to help? What kinds of systems of support would they like to see? They may wish to record their views in a short article or contribute to a debate on this issue.
- Students can consider the statement: 'There is no need for families any more' and debate this in the group.
- Students can consider the statement: 'Parents should stay together for the sake of their children rather than being selfish and leaving them in order to take up with a new partner' or the statement: 'Divorce is wrong'.
- Family detectives – use some of the 'snapshot' cards from Session 3 or devise your own similar ones to describe children from complex families. Ask the students to work out (for example) how someone could have four mums, be white but have a black sister or be older then their uncle.

Joe's Family

My home

I live with my mum and my sister, Kim, in the same house we've always lived in. This is my home because I've got my own bedroom and all my things here. My dad moved out when I was four. Sometimes Kim and I used to visit Dad in his new flat. Then Dad met Tracey. She's got three children all younger than me. Dad and Tracey have bought a new house together and now they've got a baby too. Kim and I visit Dad and Tracey once every month. Dad says we've got two homes but I have to sleep on the sofa when we go there so I don't think it is really home.

My family

I've got a mum and a dad and I've got a kid sister and I've got a step-mum and two step brothers and a step sister and a half sister. I've got three grandparents still alive… and Tracey's mum is a step-gran but she treats me and Kim just the same as Tracey's kids at birthdays and stuff so she's like a real gran. I've got four aunts on my dad's side and an uncle on my mum's side. I don't know how many cousins I've got.

The good things about my life are…

I get lots of presents at Christmas and birthdays.

I'm used to being with different people so I'm not shy.

My family all love me.

The bad things about my life are…

Sometimes I wish Mum and Dad were still together.

Sometimes I worry about my mum – I think she's lonely.

I'm not sure if Tracey really likes me and Kim.

My Home and Family

My home

....
....
....
....
....

My family

....
....
....
....
....

The good things about my life are...

....
....
....
....
....

The bad things about my life are...

....
....
....
....
....

How Others Feel

A woman of 45 whose husband has just left her for a girl of 19.

A child whose father has just left home in order to set up home with his new girlfriend.

A mother whose partner has decided that he is gay.

A child whose best friend's parents have just split up.

A child who has just found out his mother is having an affair.

A child who has gone to live with his father whilst his sister has stayed with his mother.

A child who has been put into foster care whilst her parents divorce.

A father whose partner has taken all the children to live with her new partner and will not give him access without a fight.

Feeling Connected

Fill in the diagram to show all the people you are connected to. This can be family, friends or neighbours. Put the people you feel closest to next to you.

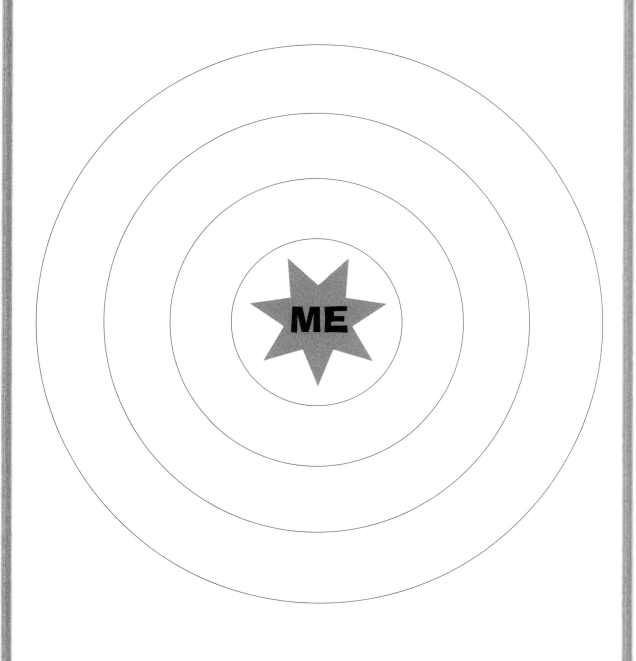

Session 3
Belonging

Introduction

For this session the facilitator will need to be aware of students within the group who are 'looked after', adopted or who have refugee status. It may be important to highlight the nature and content of the session to these students prior to the start of session so they can prepare themselves. You may want to ask if they feel able to contribute to the session or not. Please refer to the facilitator's checklist too.

This topic can be introduced with reference to the poem by Bertel Martin *I Am a Black Man*. We suggest you also prepare an opening statement to help normalise the focus of the session, for example:

> ...most children grow up with one or both of their 'birth' parents. Lots of children don't. Similarly, most people grow up in the country where they were born and where their extended birth family lives. Again lots of children don't. Children who grow up with people or in places where they don't belong by birth have all experienced loss. This loss may feel similar to bereavement even if no one has died. In today's session we are going to be thinking about identity and belonging and what these sorts of complex losses feel like...

Talk time

In small groups discuss the poem *I Am a Black Man*. To prompt focused discussion you may want to:

- ask them to explain in their own words what this man is trying to tell us
- think about how his experience is similar or different to people in the group

In the whole group ask students to share ideas about their discussion and feed back one thing that is the same and one thing that is different for people in their group. Key points that need to be made include:

- our identities are shaped by the people and the places that we feel we belong to
- our identity is also linked with the way we look
- we sometimes don't notice what we've got until we lose it
- this poem conveys something about feeling different, outside or even lonely.

Activity 1 – Write your own 'I am' poem

Students can use the worksheet provided to write their own 'I am' poem. These could be illustrated and a display could be made to celebrate the diverse and complex origins many classrooms now include. Of equal educational value would be the collective response of an all white, rural or middle class school. Here the facilitator skills will be needed to make two particular points:

1. Even in apparently homogenous groups there is likely to be huge diversity and hidden differences.
2. If all the gaps in the poem pertain to the same place (e.g. 'Wales') this can usefully be contrasted with the original poem, and conclusions can be drawn about what it is to feel 'at home' or answer the question, 'Who am I?'

Activity 2 – Snapshot Cards

(What does it mean? How does it feel? What can we do?)

The snapshot cards are composite stories based on real children's lives. They have been written as an aid to understanding the issue of identity and for developing empathy towards what some might consider to be 'outsiders'. The intention is that they should be used to further develop understanding of loss and change, in relation to the concept of 'belonging'. The cards also aim to challenge stereotypes and present the topic in terms of the young people as survivors not victims.

Use the snapshot cards as we have suggested here or tailor an activity to suit your particular group (see Follow-on activities too).

In preparation for this session write the terms listed on the worksheet 'Definitions' on flip-chart paper. Explain to the students that this is a thinking, feeling and doing (i.e. behaviour) task.

There are four parts to the activity:

1. Divide the group into pairs and give each pair one card. Ask them to imagine this person moves next door to you and/or starts attending school with you. What could they do to help the young person feel welcome? Ask the students to think about how they or the school could make these children feel more welcome, comfortable, safe, included, understood and as having things in common with the majority, as well as differences.

   Feed back to the whole group and draw out general points about inclusion.

2. Individually, in pairs or in small groups, ask the students to provide definitions for the terms listed on the flip-chart. In the whole group check definitions and then list the sorts of losses that people with these experiences have had (home, country, 'normal family', childhood as we think it should be, friends, death, etc.)

3. Using the flip-chart, brainstorm feelings words to describe feelings specific to these experiences. While we cannot know exactly how one person with this experience might feel, it is possible to empathise and identify patterns. Typically, people with these experiences could feel: different, lonely, left out, unaccepted, misunderstood, outside, excluded, outnumbered (minority), unsafe, frightened, unwelcome or inferior.

   They may also be bullied for their differences and/or may try to hide things about themselves from other people. Sometimes children with these sorts of experiences will develop 'passing' strategies to hide their differences.

4. Finally, in order to reinforce learning, ask students to work in pairs or small groups to complete an individual worksheet 'Definitions'.

You could display individual responses to 'What can I do?' as a way to raise the profile of how the school can work to improve the inclusion of minority students.

Please note: the 'feelings' words that are identified in this activity will mirror the ones identified in Session 1 Activity 3 and you should refer back to that work to link this session with the main work of the programme.

This activity could be extended through reference to topical news items and real life personal 'survivor' stories (see follow-on activities below).

Activity 3 – Get packing

Use the worksheet 'Get Packing' and ask the students to illustrate what they would like to be able to take with them if they were a refugee and had to leave home quickly. Or ask the students to illustrate a poem or real life survivor story.

Plenary

The facilitator can ask students to brainstorm the following question, 'What have we learnt about refugees and those in care and the way in which they experience loss?' Responses can be recorded on the flip-chart whilst you highlight the following key points:

- It is important to gain accurate information and knowledge about such students/groups.
- It is important to provide and be part of appropriate support systems which do not patronise but ensure their inclusion.
- Overall, it is essential to highlight the fact that such individuals have equal rights in terms of having their losses and grief acknowledged and having their needs met within the context in which they currently find themselves.

You may want to introduce next week's topic during the plenary and to ask students to think of any questions they would like to ask about death.

Follow-on activities

On the move

Use recent newspaper articles as the starting point for some work on attitudes to 'outsiders'. Students can collect articles about refugees and their experiences. These can be sorted into two groups – those which illustrate positive and inclusive experience and those which illustrate a negative and exclusive experience. A display could be made.

It may be helpful to arrange for an adult with refugee status and an adult who has had experience of the care system to come into the group and discuss their experiences. Students may wish to draw up a series of questions prior to these visits in order to make the most of them.

'The personal is political' – discuss in relation to the issue of inter-country adoption.

Write an essay entitled 'Home is where the heart is' – discuss.

Personal stories

Collect personal stories from papers and magazines or from within the school to make into a resource for use throughout the school.

Victim or survivor

Discuss in relation to any of the snapshot cards or real life stories you collect. List all the changes and losses the person has experienced. Give each loss a score according to whether it is a big loss or a small loss. Have a go at ranking the stories according to these scores. (Please note this is neither possible nor desirable! Some sort of 'more or less' spectrum may emerge and an interesting discussion will take place.) Compare this to your own life and losses you have experienced. Think about whether the person has gained anything as well. Are there any positive parts to the story, and if so do they compensate for the losses?

Imagine you are the person in this snapshot and you are granted three wishes. Name your wishes and explain why you have chosen them.

Draw a picture to illustrate one of the snapshot cards.

Write a letter to one of the young people described in the snapshot card.

Make a poster to encourage people to donate money to a charity raising money for people in this sort of situation.

Useful organisations

British Association for Adoption and Fostering (BAAF)

Saffron House

6-10 Kirby Street

London

EC1N 8TS

Telephone: 020 7421 2600

www.baaf.org.uk

Amnesty International

Amnesty International UK

The Human Rights Action Centre

17-25 New Inn Yard

London

EC2A 3EA

Telephone: 020 7033 1500

Fax: 020 7033 1503

Textphone: 020 7033 1664

Email: sct@amnesty.org.uk

www.amnesty.org.uk

Winston's Wish

The Clara Burgess Centre

Bayshill Rd

Cheltenham

Gloucestershire

GL50 3AW

www.winstonswish.org.uk

Refugee Council

Refugee Council Head Office

240-250 Ferndale Road

London SW9 8BB

Telephone: 020 7346 6700

Fax: 020 7346 6701

www.refugeecouncil.org.uk

The Child Bereavement Trust

Aston House

West Wycombe

High Wycombe

Bucks

HP14 3AG

Telephone: 01494 446648

Fax: 01494 440057

Email: enquiries@childbereavement.org.uk

www.childbereavement.org.uk

Big Issue Foundation

1-2 Wandsworth Road

London

SW8 2LN

Telephone: 020 7526 3252

www.bigissue.com

I Am a Black Man

I am a Black man.

My soul is in Afrika,

my mind is on the West Indies,

my feet are in England.

I am a Black man.

My spirit is in Afrika,

my heart is in the West Indies,

my body is in England.

I am a Black man.

My ancestors are in Afrika,

my relations in the West Indies,

my family in England.

I am a MAN.

My history is of Afrika,

my past is of the West Indies,

my present is of England,

my future is of the world.

Bertel Martin

© Bertel Martin, 1992

Reproduced with permission of the author

Write Your Own 'I Am' Poem

I Am...

I am a _____

My soul _____

my mind is on the _____

my feet are in _____

I am a _____

My spirit is in _____

my heart is in _____

my body is in _____

I am a _____

My ancestors are in_____

my relations in the _____

my family in_____.

I am a _____

My history is of _____

my past is of the _____

my present is of _____

my future is of _____.

Definitions

What does it mean?

Term	Definition
Looked after	....
In care	....
Fostered	....
Adopted	....
Transracially adopted	....
Inter-country adopted	....
Immigrant	....
Emigrant	....
Asylum seeker	....
Refugee	....
Homeless	....
Excluded	....
Traveller	....
Disabled	....
Dual-heritage	....
Mixed race	....

How does it feel?

What feelings might be common to people with these experiences?

What can we do?

How could you make people with these experiences feel more welcome, included, comfortable or safe?

Snapshot Cards

Danny is 14 and is living in a children's home with two other boys. He is 'looked after' by social services. His father is Greek and lives in Greece. Danny has not seen him since he was 6. Danny's mum is a heroin user and cannot keep Danny safe at home. Danny has been excluded from school and is often in trouble with the police.

Louise is 17. Her mum died when she was five. She is from Kent originally but she ran away from her violent and alchoholic father when she was 14. She lives on the streets in Manchester. She begs in the day and sometimes she sleeps in shelters at night. She's got good friends who also live on the streets and some of them sell the *Big Issue*.

Wan was born in China but because of the one child policy, her parents put her in an orphanage when she was a baby. At six months old she was adopted by a white English family living in Yorkshire. Wan is now 13 and happy in her family but she is the only Chinese girl in her school.

Mina is from Bosnia. In 1992, when she was 13, Mina's family were all killed by Serb soldiers. She escaped to Croatia and was then moved to a refugee camp in Slovenia. After two years she was allowed to come and live in England. Mina is now at university and plans to return to Bosnia when she has finished her degree.

Kelly's mum has mental health difficulties and her father is in prison. Her step-father sexually abused her between the age of 10 and 13 and she was taken into care by her social worker. She is now living with foster carers. Kelly will be taking her GCSEs this year and hopes to go to college next year to do a child-care qualification.

Gemma is 15 and has not attended school for two years. Sometimes she has home education but most days she hangs around the shopping centre with older friends or other pupils who have been excluded. Gemma would like to go to college and get her exams. She doesn't want to go to school because she got bullied and then excluded for getting into fights.

Snapshot Cards (cont.)

S3

Jacob was born in England and is 'dual-heritage'. His mum is from Tunisia and is Muslim. His dad is British Jamaican; was brought up as a Christian, but has now converted to Islam. Jacob is 14 years old and goes to his local school. Next year his parents are planning to take Jacob and his sister to Tunisia to live. Jacob is not sure if he wants to live in Tunisia.

Naz is 16 and at college. She has lived in England all her life but her parents are from Pakistan originally. Naz's parents died in a car crash last year and she is living with an aunt and uncle. Naz doesn't get on with them because they are very strict. Her uncle says he will send her to live with relatives in Pakistan if she doesn't do what he says.

Donna is 13 and was transracially adopted when she was two. Her birth mother was white and her birth father was black. She lives with her adoptive mum and dad, who are both teachers. Donna goes to school in a multi-cultural area but her best friends are all white. She plans to go to university and train to be a Doctor.

Parvan is 14. He is the only Sikh in his school which is a Catholic School in Brighton. Parvan lives with his parents, his grandmother and his two sisters. There are very few other pupils in the school who live with both their parents. There are also very few children in the school who regularly practice their religion. Parvan has never been invited to a sleepover.

Sam is 14 and has got four mums and two homes! His birth-mother Carole is a lesbian who used artificial insemination to conceive Sam. Until he was four he lived with Carole and her partner Kay. When they split up, Kay moved in with her new partner, Dee. Sam's mum now lives with her new partner Caroline. Sam does not dare tell his girlfriend about his unusual family.

Paul is 15 years old, lives with his parents and attends his local comprehensive school, where he has lots of friends. He is physically disabled and uses a wheelchair. He travels to school in a special taxi and is able to access all classes except PE. Next year Paul will have to go to a special residential college to do his A levels because his local college is not wheelchair accessible.

Snapshot Cards (cont.)

Brendan is 13 and lives in a caravan with his parents. They move around the country getting work at fairgrounds and festivals. Sometimes Brendan attends a local school. At other times a teacher comes to the travellers' site and gives home education. Although he sometimes gets bullied for being different, Brendan loves being a traveller and plans to live like this all his life.

Jordan is white and 12 years old and moved to England from the USA last year. He now lives in London with his parents where he attends the local comprehensive school. Jordan's mum is British and his father is American. Jordan has made new friends in England and likes his school, but he still thinks of America as home.

Halima is 13 and is originally from Somalia. Her parents fled Somalia because of religious persecution when she was six months old. They took her to live in a refugee camp in Kenya, where sadly her father died. After six years, the U.N. gave permission for Halima and her mother to come to live in England, where she now attends her local comprehensive. Halima is a shy person and has not made any friends yet.

Selemani was five years old when he saw both his parents murdered in Rwanda. He was taken to a refugee camp in Zaire where he lived for three years. He was then adopted by a French couple who have since settled in England. Selemani's first language is Kinyarwanda; he also speaks French and English. Although he has missed a lot of education, Selemani hopes to go to college soon.

Jason has special educational needs; he has ADHD and has Ritalin on prescription. He also has literacy difficulties and finds it hard to concentrate. He has got good friends out of school but in school he is often on his own at break. Teachers seem to pick on him and he often gets bullied for not being able to read as well as most of the pupils in his class.

Get Packing

Sometimes refugees have to leave their homes with very little warning.

They have to pack their bags quickly.

Imagine you have to pack your suitcase and leave your home. What would you like to take with you? Draw in the suitcase or write underneath it.

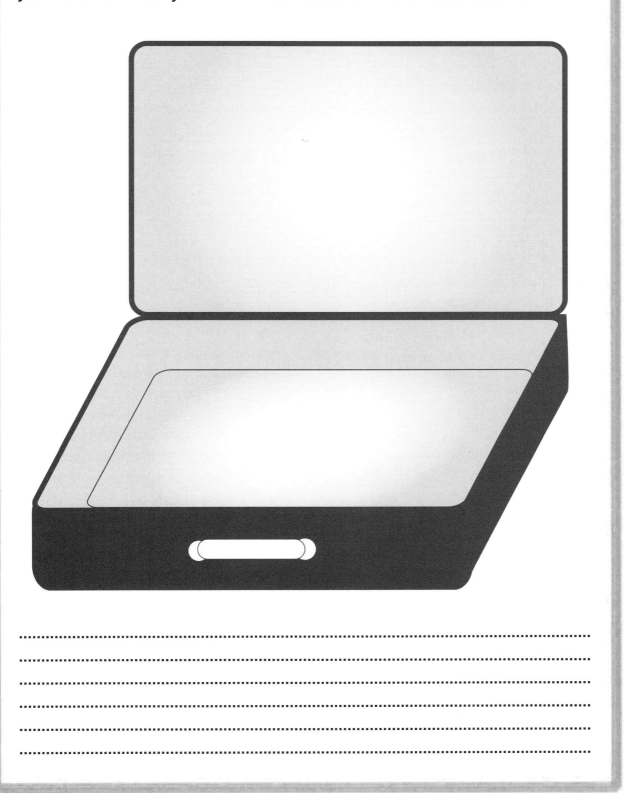

....
....
....
....
....
....

Session 4
A Matter of Life and Death

Introduction

This session introduces the core work of the programme, that of death. The aim is to promote a more open attitude to death and dying which will allow pupils to begin to share their knowledge and concerns around death and to ask questions they may not have previously been able to voice. Consideration must be given to the way different religious beliefs will influence how willing pupils may feel to join in some parts of this session. Similarly, pupils recently or otherwise bereaved may need to be forewarned of the content of today's session.

Talk time

Use the cartoon 'Kicked The Bucket' to introduce this session. Ask the pupils to brainstorm all the different euphemisms for death and/or summarise by showing the handout which lists many common euphemisms. You may want to make the following points:

- euphemisms are often used for taboo subjects such as death as a way of avoiding really talking about it
- children can get confused and even scared by euphemisms, they may take things literally
- euphemisms teach us from an early age that death cannot be talked about openly.

Now open the discussion out and ask the group why death is taboo. Summarise the discussion plus you may wish to include some of the following points:

- The difficulty we have with talking about death doesn't seem to apply in the media and computer games. We develop a stereotype of death as violent, and traumatic, so we do not develop a vocabulary for talking about more ordinary ways of dying.
- Death is not encountered as directly as in past times and other cultures.
- We do not always live near close family.
- We are protected from death by doctors and hospitals.
- Science has reduced infant mortality and there is a greater expectation that technology can save us.
- There is an overall reduction in religious belief and, as such, less concern with the afterlife. Death is viewed as final rather than as moving on to a reward or punishment for what we have done in life.
- There has been a decline in the rituals around death. Death is not marked in the same ways. Children often don't attend funerals. Just one member of a family living long distances apart may attend a funeral.

Activity 1 – Life expectancy

Use the quotation from the Bible, Ecclesiastes, Chapter 3, Verses 1-8 as a prompt. Copies could be provided.

This passage posits that there is a time for everything and that everything will come to an end. Students can then be asked to consider how every living thing must have a limited lifespan and the ways in which some lifespans are more limited than others. They can use the worksheet 'Lifespans' and work in pairs or in small groups in order to formulate lists of different objects and animals, etc. This could include animals, machinery such as CD players, televisions, clothes, people, etc. The students can then identify how long they think many of these things will last and compare notes with each other. The idea here is to reinforce this concept of the transitory nature of life and the fact that it does usually have a beginning, middle and an end. What happens after life is something that can be considered later but at this point the focus is on the fact that all human beings and objects will have a life expectancy which may be either short or long and dependent upon certain contextual factors.

It would also be helpful to consider what the current average life expectancy is in the country and the ways in which people curtail or promote their life expectancy.

Activity 2 – Media representations of death

For this activity the facilitator can collect a range of newspapers and magazine articles which focus on the topic of death. Alternatively, ask the students to bring in articles themselves. Students can work in pairs to make collages from these articles picking out the most significant stories, ideas and concepts for themselves. This can be done as a group task and each group can then feed back to the whole group in terms of their own impressions as to how death is portrayed in the media and whether or not they always agree with the way in which people write about and present death.

Students may wish to consider which types of death get most cover in the media and to question why this might be the case. They could also discuss how certain disasters are reported and written about and whether or not the vocabulary and language is similar. They may consider how media reporting of a person's death or accident can and does impact on family and friends who are left behind.

Activity 3 – Any questions?

In small groups ask the students to come up with a list of questions about death and dying. Feed back to the larger group and make a list. Try to group the questions in ways that are meaningful to your group. These could be:

- Information/factual – What happens in a morgue? Why do some cultures wear black and some white at a funeral? What do people look like when dead? Is cancer contagious?
- Philosophical – why do people commit suicide? Is there life after death?
- Statistical – numbers, different types of death, causes.
- Risk-taking – drugs, alcohol (Can you die from...? How do you tell if...?)
- Support – what can you say to someone who is terminally ill or whose mum has just died?

The co-facilitator should scribe for the group so that you have a record of this discussion for future reference. Allow students to discuss the questions and even explore answers. Emphasise that the focus is on the questions. Explain that over the next few weeks you hope to help the students answer some of these questions, clarify misconceptions and or help them to arrive at their own conclusions.

Make sure you adapt your future planning to include the sort of content that has been raised here. Similarly, refer back to the notes you made in Session 1 Plenary. Use materials in the follow-on activities section to help you do this.

Plenary

To review the learning that has taken place in this session, ask the students: 'What do we know about death?' This can be done as a whole group discussion and recorded on a flip-chart. To some extent, the discussion will mirror the introduction. You may want to clarify the use of euphemisms, and the idea of death being a taboo subject. You could also summarise ways in which the media presents death. Finally, you can identify significant concerns/issues/questions that students may have regarding death and dying.

Follow-on activities

Students can choose to either draw or write their own life expectancy path. It might be interesting for students to share these with each other by presenting them as a display.

Students could illustrate the bible quotation.

Students can think about how our perceptions of death may change through time. Refer to the children's understanding of death in the introduction. They can focus on the following questions:

- How did we think about death when we were younger?
- How do we now think about death?

It may be helpful to provide the students with examples in order to prompt discussion. The facilitator may wish to highlight the following points:

- Students are consistently bombarded with images of death on the news and in the media as a whole.
- When they are young, children tend to gain some rather odd perceptions of death due to this kind of imagery and due to their experiences, particularly in the area of games and playground activities which involve death e.g. cowboys and Indians, cops and robbers, playing hospitals, etc. It can be hard for a young child to make the distinction between the death on a television programme and something that is reported in the news, which is actually real. It is also quite easy to see how younger children can have some misconceptions of death when they very often tend to take things more literally than adults do. For example, a child may be told that a statue is a representation of Princess Diana who has been dead for quite a few years now. The child may then begin to think that all people who die will turn into statues.

Illustrate in cartoon style a given number of the euphemisms from the handout.

Kicked the Bucket

Kicked the Bucket – Euphemisms

Passed away

Passed over

Passed on

Fell asleep

Didn't wake up

Snuffed it

Kicked the bucket

Popped his clogs

Laid to rest

No longer with us

Crossed over

Curtains

The final call

Pushing up daisies

Promoted

Lost

Gone

Not able to save him/her

Taken/Taken by God/Allah

Gone to live with the angels

In heaven/paradise

With granny (or someone else who has died)

Gone to a better place

Gone to meet her maker

Put her/him down (of animals)

At the happy hunting ground

Life Expectancy

'There is an appointed time for everything, and a time for every affair under the heavens.

A time to be born, and a time to die: a time to plant, and a time to uproot the plant.

A time to kill, and a time to heal: a time to tear down, and a time to build.

A time to weep, and a time to laugh: a time to mourn, and a time to dance.

A time to scatter stones, and a time to gather them; a time to embrace, and a time to be far from embraces.

A time to seek, and a time to lose; a time to keep, and a time to cast away.

A time to read, and a time to sew; a time to be silent, and a time to speak.

A time to love, and a time to hate: a time of war, and a time of peace.'

The New American Bible – Ecclesiastes, Chapter 3, Verses 1-8.

Lifespans

Work in pairs or small groups and make a list of different objects or living things. Think about how these will begin, how they will end and how long they have lasted. Compare your notes with other groups.

○ ....
  ....
  ....

○ ....
  ....
  ....

○ ....
  ....
  ....

○ ....
  ....
  ....

○ ....
  ....
  ....

○ ....
  ....
  ....

S4

Session 5
Facts and Figures

Introduction

The aim of this session is to increase students' vocabulary of death and dying and knowledge of statistics about how, when and why people die. The idea here is to highlight the many and varied ways that people encounter death – it is not necessarily a dramatic or horrific event. Sometimes, death may occur quite naturally at the end of an individual's long and healthy life. At other times, someone may suffer terribly prior to a death which is prompted by a terminal illness, e.g. cancer. Some deaths may be caused by natural disasters, accidents or suicide. It is important for students to be aware of the range of causes and to have access to accurate and unsensationalised information and statistics.

Talk time

Students can be divided into four groups and provided with the 'Death' worksheet. The students can then be asked to:

- Brainstorm all the words they associate with death. The facilitator can give examples such as 'funeral' and 'morgue'. While this is not a 'feelings word' activity, if students come up with words such as 'grief' that's fine. However, it will be important that these words are picked up in Session 7.

- Students can work on a definition of death. Definitions may refer to the end of life, a finishing off time, a natural stillness, etc. Students can feed back their own definitions to the group as a whole and compare responses and ideas, identifying any similarities and differences.

Activity 1 – The A-Z of death and dying

Students can be asked to either make their own dictionary of words associated with death (based on their brainstorm activity) or complete the worksheet 'A to Z of Death and Dying'. Use the facilitator's reference sheet to help.

Dictionaries and thesauruses can be used for this activity. It will be appropriate to have a range of reference material, including IT based resources, to ensure that all students can participate regardless of ability or recording skills.

Activity 2 – Death by numbers

Students can brainstorm the many different ways in which people can die. For example:

- Hit and run
- Illness
- Epidemic illness – AIDS
- Organ failure
- Drugs
- Road accidents
- Suicide
- Murder

- Mass tragedies
- War and conflict
- Hunger/poverty
- Old age
- Natural disasters.

Ask students to work in pairs and rank the causes of death from most common to the least common cause.

It may be helpful to use the Internet to research statistics on death, or use the 'Death by Numbers' information sheet. It may then be useful to discuss the accuracy or otherwise of students' ideas here. What are the most common causes of death? Are there any differences between older and younger people and between the males and females? For example, do more young men commit suicide than older men? Do older people die of cancer more frequently than younger people? Students can identify any of the statistics, which may have surprised or shocked them, alongside those which may have confirmed views already held.

Activity 3 – Facts and figures quiz

Use the 'Facts and Figures Quiz' to check students' learning. This activity could be done orally with the students in groups, like a pub quiz, or as a written test individually, in pairs or in small teams. The facilitator will need to decide on the most appropriate delivery, taking into account the nature of the group as a whole and available time left in the session.

Plenary

The facilitator can ask students to summarise their own perceptions of death and encourage them to articulate personal definitions and ideas with particular reference to the facts and figures learnt in this session. It may be helpful to ask the following questions:

- What facts and figures about death have surprised you?
- What facts about death have shocked you?
- What facts about death have worried you?
- What facts about death have made you feel secure?

These can be recorded by the facilitator on the flip-chart in order to provide a summary of the points covered in the session and a summary of individual perceptions and views. These can be presented as key points and the facilitator can highlight any similarities and differences in students' responses.

Follow-on activities

Ask students to research statistics on historical or geographical distribution 'patterns' of death or statistical facts on one type of death (e.g. AIDS, infant mortality). Make a display with graphs, analysis and social commentary. Use of the Internet as a research tool will be helpful here. It may also be useful for students to work in small groups on this activity and to devise a 5-10 minute presentation of their work which can then be presented.

Students could focus on how to live longer and how to prevent or reduce the risk of death, i.e. how a healthy lifestyle may prevent a range of serious illnesses such as cancer, diabetes or heart disease and consequently extend life and reduce the risk of an early, unwarranted death.

Death

What do you think? What words do you associate with the word death?

The A – Z of Death and Dying
Facilitator's reference sheet

After-life	–	life after death
Bequeath	–	to leave by will
Bereavement	–	to be deprived by death
Burial	–	the placing of a body in the ground
Cemetery	–	a graveyard where coffins or caskets can be buried
Coffin	–	a (usually) wooden box in which the dead person is placed for a funeral
Corpse	–	a dead body
Cremation	–	to burn a dead body
Death	–	the act of dying, the end of life
Deceased	–	a dead person
Embalm	–	to preserve a dead body with oils and spices
Epitaph	–	words written on a tombstone or monument
Eulogy	–	to speak or write well of someone (often a speech at a funeral)
Euthanasia	–	helping people to die
Funeral	–	a ceremony for someone who has died
Funeral parlour	–	the place where a dead person's body is viewed in its coffin by family
Grave	–	a place where cremated ashes or a body is buried
Grief	–	distress, sadness or great unhappiness (usually when someone has died)
Hearse	–	a vehicle for carrying a coffin in
Immortal	–	living forever
Lament	–	an extreme expression of grief
Mausoleum	–	a grand monument

The A – Z of Death and Dying (cont.)

Memorial	–	something by which we can remember
Mortuary	–	a place in which dead bodies are placed before a funeral
Morbid	–	diseased, unhealthy (often used as gloomy and death related)
Mortal	–	destined to die
Mourning	–	to feel or express sorrow. 'In mourning' – a period following a death where particular customs may be observed (e.g. wearing dark clothes)
Mummify	–	to preserve a corpse by embalming and drying
Murder	–	unlawful killing
Obituary	–	the printed announcement of someone's death
Orphan	–	a child with one or, both parents dead
Reincarnation	–	to live again in a different body
Resurrection	–	to rise from the dead
R.I.P.	–	Rest in Peace
Soul	–	part of the human that is separate from the body and linked to God
Spirit	–	that which gives 'life' to our physical bodies
Suicide	–	to take one's own life. To kill oneself
Terminal illness	–	an illness which will end with death
Thanatology	–	the scientific study of death and the process of death
Tomb	–	a grave
Tombstone	–	a stone put up to mark a grave (also 'headstone')
Undertaker	–	a person whose job is to organise funerals

The A – Z of Death and Dying (cont.)

Wake	–	a celebration of a person's life the night before a funeral, traditionally held in their house with an open coffin to pay your respects
Widow	–	woman whose husband is dead
Widower	–	man whose wife is dead
Will	–	instructions about what to do with one's possessions at death.

Other phrases and terminology

Last will and testament	–	the usually written last statement on what to do with the dead person's belongings and/or requests regarding conditions and actions.
No flowers please. Donations to…	–	usually in an announcement about a funeral reflecting the wishes of the dead person regarding how they want people to say goodbye.
Organ donor	–	someone who has agreed to give bits of their body to doctors usually after their death.

The A – Z of Death and Dying

What do these words mean? Use a dictionary to help you.

After-life ....

Bereavement ....

Burial ....

Cemetery ....

Coffin ....

Corpse ....

Cremation ....

Death ....

Deceased ....

Euthanasia ....

Funeral ....

Grave ....

Grief ....

The A – Z of Death and Dying (cont..)

Hearse ....

Memorial ....

Mortuary ....

Mourning ....

Murder ....

Obituary ....

Orphan ....

Reincarnation ....

R.I.P. ....

Soul ....

Spirit ....

Suicide ....

Thanatology ....

Undertaker ....

Wake ....

Widow ....

Widower ....

Will ....

Death By Numbers

'We owe respect to the living; to the dead we owe only truth'.   Voltaire

UK Death statistics 2002

Smoking	106,000
Other accidental deaths	8,579
Alcoholic liver disease	5,121
Suicide	4,066
Traffic accidents	3,439
Poisoning and overdose	881
Murder and manslaughter	513

Cancer

A quarter (26%) of all people who die in the UK each year die from cancer.

A third (37%) of deaths under 65 are caused by cancer.

Smoking

106,000 people in the UK are killed by smoking each year.

One fifth of all deaths in the UK are caused by smoking.

Half of all teenagers who are currently smoking will die from smoking related diseases.

Coronary Heart Disease (CHD) and Obesity

In 2002 117,500 people died from heart disease – 42,500 of these were premature deaths.

Smoking and obesity are two of the main causes of heart disease.

28% of girls and 22 % of boys are obese (in 1995 these figures were 22% and 16%).

Death By Numbers (cont.)

HIV and AIDS

Worldwide – In 2004, 3.1 million died from AIDS (2.6 adults 0.5 children) and 15 million children were orphaned by AIDS in 2003.

In the UK there have been 21,280 cases of AIDS and at least 13,145 people have died.

In 2004 6403 new cases of HIV infection were diagnosed. More than 50% of recent diagnoses have been in heterosexual men and women.

Suicide

Every two hours, someone in Britain commits suicide.

Worldwide about 1000 people commit suicide every day or one each minute.

Suicide is the most common cause of death for men aged 15-44 years.

Men are three times more likely to commit suicide than women.

In the last 30 years, suicide rates have doubled for 15-24 year olds.

Drug Related Deaths

In 1996 the following figures for drug related deaths in the UK were recorded

Methadone	357
Heroin	187
Temazepan	95
Amphetamine	29
Cocaine crack	15
Ecstasy	12
Cannabis	4
LSD	0

3% of people die from illegal drug-related deaths.

Death By Numbers (cont.)

Murder

The countries with the highest number of murders are:

Columbia 0.63 per 100   South Africa 0.51   Jamaica 0.32.

In the US this drops to less than one in 10,000 and in the UK one in 100,000.

Most murders are committed by someone known to the victim.

Accidents

Every year more than 3,000 people die from traffic accidents in the UK. Other accidental deaths account for a further 8-9,000 deaths.

The most common form of death for teenagers is by car accident.

Poverty

Every 3 seconds a child dies because they happen to be born poor. This amounts to 30,000 each day.

War, Mass Murder and Genocide

During World War 2 Nazis were responsible for the deaths of 63% of the European Jewish population, approximately 6,000,000 people.

The post-WWII policies and actions of Joseph Stalin in Communist Russia, resulted in the death of an estimated 30 million people in the Soviet Union, over an 8 year period to 1953.

In 1994 the Hutu majority in Rwanda organised and implemented the mass slaughter of the Tutsi minority. In just 100 days 800,000 people were killed.

Capital Punishment in the UK

13th July 1955 – Ruth Ellis becomes the last woman to be hanged in England.

15th August 1963 – The last hanging in Scotland was that of 21-year-old Henry Burnett.

December 1969 – Parliament confirmed abolition of capital punishment for murder.

1998 – Death penalty abolished for crimes committed under military jurisdiction.

Death By Numbers (cont.)

Capital Punishment in the USA

Capital punishment is still practised in 19 states and is still legal in 38.

In 1999, 98 prisoners were executed.

Natural Disasters

About quarter of a million people died in the Asian Tsunami on 26 December 2004.

About 10,000 people die each year in earthquakes.

Worldwide, about 5,000 people are struck by lightening each year. Of these, about 20% or 1000 will die.

Every year about 1500 city dwellers in America die of heat.

Strange But True

Vets are four times more likely to commit suicide than any other profession.

You are more likely to die crossing the road than in an aeroplane crash.

May is the month when most suicides happen.

In the UK 24 people will be struck by lightening each year. 5 will die.

Every year about 100 people die from choking on ball point pens.

Every year more than 2,500 left-handed people are killed from using right-handed products.

Facts and Figures Quiz

1. Thanatology means:

a) death

b) the study of death

c) the study of illness.

2. An obituary is:

a) a written account of someones life

b) a funeral speech

c) a type of biscuit.

3) An epitaph is:

a) a dying person's last words

b) a dying person's last request

c) words written on a tombstone.

4) Euthanasia means:

a) a lung disease

b) suicide

c) assisted death.

5) A mortuary is:

a) a place where dead bodies are placed before a funeral

b) a funeral parlour

c) a wake.

6. To live forever, means to:

a) be mortal

b) be immortal

c) to be embalmed.

Facts and Figures Quiz (cont.)

7. A man whose wife has died is called:

a) a widow

b) a window

c) a widower.

8. What fraction of the population who die in the UK each year, die from cancer?

a) one third

b) a quarter

c) a fifth.

9. What fraction of all deaths in the UK are caused by smoking?

a) one third

b) a quarter

c) a fifth.

10. With what disease is obesity linked?

a) cancer

b) coronary heart disease

c) depression.

11. Of recent HIV diagnoses about what percentage have been heterosexual men and women?

a) less than 50%

b) More than 50%

c) About 5%.

12. Which group of people is most likely to commit suicide?

a) Women aged 20-24 years

b) Men aged 15-44 years

c) Men aged 60-74 years.

Facts and Figures Quiz (cont.)

13. The death penalty was abolished in the UK in:

a) 1966

b) 1996

c) 1969.

14. The percentage of people who die of drug related deaths, from illegal drug use is:

a) 3%

b) 30%

c) 33%.

15. Most murders are committed by:

a) complete strangers

b) someone known to the victim

c) foreigners.

16. The most common form of death for teenagers is by:

a) car accident

b) bike accident

c) poisoning.

17. A child dies from poverty related causes every:

a) 3 seconds

b) 3 minutes

c) 3 hours.

Facts and Figures Quiz (cont.)

18. About how many Jewish people were killed in World War 2?

a) 6,000

b) 60,000

c) 6,000,000.

19. About how many people died in the Asian Tsunami in December 2004?

a) 25,000

b) 250,000

c) 125,000.

20. What percentage of people who are struck by lightening actually die?

a) 50%

b) 10%

c) 20%.

Answers

1.b)   2.a)   3.c)   4.c)   5.a)   6.b)   7.c)   8.b)   9.c)   10.b)   11.b)   12.b)
13.c)   14.a)   15.b)   16.a)   17.b)   18.a)   19.b)   20.c)

Session 6
Beliefs and Customs

Introduction

This session will help students to gain a more in-depth understanding of death. The session will reinforce the statistics and help students understand how our concept of death varies according to our culture and religion. During this session students are encouraged to explore their own views on 'life after death', alongside the afterlife beliefs, death rituals and funeral customs of the major world religions. As preparation for this session, teachers should read the 'World Religions' facilitator's notes.

The facilitator could use examples of religious art and artefacts depicting heaven and hell as a way of introducing this session. These can be found in the visual arts section of public and school libraries and could include artefacts from the ancient religions, as well as paintings and sculptures depicting the afterlife beliefs of the major world religions.

Talk time

As usual, the group rules will need to be reinforced. It may also be useful to clarify the need to show respect to different cultures and belief systems.

Ask the students, in pairs or small groups, to discuss the nine statements provided on the handout 'Is There Life After Death?'. Then invite the pairs or small groups to feed back the key points of their discussion to the whole group.

It should be stressed that these are individual responses, and their own thoughts and feelings are specific to themselves. These will be influenced by cultural and religious backgrounds and it is important to be respectful of difference. The example sheet contains the following nine statements:

1. I think someone should die and then come back to life so that they could tell us what it was really like once you are dead.
2. There is no such thing as death, you just come back as another spirit or another person and live on.
3. I believe that there are souls and that they live on for ever and ever, but bodies give up because they get old and tired.
4. Death is scary because there is nothing else after it and we don't understand it. What you don't understand is frightening.
5. Everything has to die at some time; that is just nature.
6. Being buried is not a good thing because you just rot away. It seems better to me to be burnt and then you can go back into the air.
7. I think that there is a God and heaven and hell and that when you die you either go to one or the other.
8. I think there is a human life force that comes from an eternal energy but I don't think it's God, I think it is something else.
9. When you are dead that's it; it's final and you cannot think or feel anymore.

Activity 1 – Spread the word

Divide the students into seven small groups and give each group a handout on one of the major world religions and beliefs. Ask them to read and discuss the handout.

Each group represents a different religion and should complete the worksheet 'World Religions'. Bring all of the groups back together and mix them up into two or more new groups, so that there is at least one representative of the seven religions in each of the newly formed groups. In turn, members of the new groups share the information about their religion with the others. Students can start to complete the worksheet 'Beliefs and Customs of the World Religions' but could then reconvene with their original group to complete it.

Activity 2 – Burial or cremation

During the first half of this century it was generally tradition to bury the deceased. However, during the past twenty to thirty years the majority of people in this country have opted for cremation although there still exists many religious groups who object to this form of disposal of the body. Orthodox Jews and Muslims will not be cremated whilst in India the tradition has always been to cremate the dead.

In this activity, students will be provided with the worksheet in which they can record both the advantages and disadvantages of burial and cremation. It may be helpful, prior to completion of this task, if students are allowed some time to talk about these issues and discuss their views with both the facilitator and members of their peer group. It may also be helpful for the facilitator to highlight some of the advantages and disadvantages of both forms of disposal. For example, advantages of burial could include the fact that graves could be visited once the person has been buried and this may give a lot of comfort to those who are left behind. This also makes for a more personal form of grieving. Disadvantages of burial include the fact that it is much more expensive and can also be quite upsetting for some members of the family. Also, it can be quite difficult for some family members who live far away from the grave to actually get over to visit it when they feel they would most like to.

Some of the advantages of cremation may include the fact that it is cheaper and perhaps more hygienic. It can save land and enables those who are left behind to remember the person later, i.e. by scattering their ashes somewhere special or personal to them. One disadvantage is that many people dislike seeing the coffin rolling away in front of them. Some people may also complain that the cremation service is rather rushed and consequently feels far more impersonal than a graveside funeral.

Students can complete this activity in pairs or small groups or individually as appropriate. It would be helpful to allow some time for feedback so that the facilitator can once again elicit students' views and identify significant differences between particular groups and individuals.

Activity 3 – Make a display

Students can make a large wall display showing key similarities and differences in the beliefs and customs of the major world religions. The facilitator can include all the students in the group by asking them to produce drawings, posters and poems and to complete follow-on activities. Use this as a tool for promoting a tolerant and respectful attitude towards different religions and cultures in the school.

Plenary

Finally, the students can focus upon the following questions:

- What have we learnt in this session about the beliefs and customs surrounding death ideas about life after death?
- How do our thoughts and feeling differ and what are the similarities in our views and perceptions?

The facilitator can record students' views, feelings and thoughts using the flip-chart as a series of key points in order to provide a summary and reinforce the concepts covered.

Follow-on activities

Students can find out about life after death beliefs from a range of different faiths and civilisations, e.g. Muslim, Egypt, Greek, Jewish, etc.

Students can discuss the notion of ghosts and whether or not this would indicate any kind of life after death if there were such things. They may also wish to discuss a range of ghost stories and why the notion of an afterlife could be either a fearful thing or a comfort to people who are left behind.

Articles regarding out-of-the-body experiences could be collected and discussed and arranged as a collage for the purposes of prompting further discussion.

Students can discuss views regarding life after death with members of their family and other adults in the school community. They may wish to construct a questionnaire for this purpose.

Is There Life After Death?

In pairs, discuss the following nine statements.

Which do you agree or disagree with?

What are the arguments for and against there being a life after death?

1. I think someone should die and then come back to life so that they could tell us what it was really like once you are dead.

2. There is no such thing as death, you just come back as another spirit or another person and live on.

3. I believe that there are souls and that they live on for ever and ever, but bodies give up because they get old and tired.

4. Death is scary because there is nothing else after it and we don't understand it. What you don't understand is frightening.

5. Everything has to die at some time; that is just nature.

6. Being buried is not a good thing because you just rot away. It seems better to me to be burnt as then you can go back into the air.

7. I think that there is a God and heaven and hell and that when you die you either go to one or the other.

8. I think there is a human life force that comes from an eternal energy but I don't think it's God, I think it is something else.

9. When you are dead that's it; it's final and you cannot think or feel anymore.

World Religions

Facilitator's notes

The following pages give an overview of the most influential world religions in the UK; their different afterlife beliefs, death rituals and funeral customs. These are very general descriptions. All religions tend to evolve and adapt, according to the political social and economic climate in which they are being practised. Most religions also contain a broad range of practice and a variety of different denominations or schools of thought. Broadly speaking, most religions have an 'orthodox' or more fundamentalist tradition. Similarly, most religions include believers who have a more liberal and questioning approach, who may try to accommodate developments in science and culture.

Humanism, agnosticism, atheism and disbelief

We have included humanism as a major influential belief because often, in the West, people do not identify themselves as religious. Paradoxically, many people do not regularly attend a place of worship but may do so for a funeral. Increasing numbers of people in the West hold memorial celebrations as well as funerals, which may combine humanist elements and elements from different religions. Sometimes this is to ensure the values and beliefs of all parts of complex and multi-faith families are respected. Many people now express doubts about fundamental aspects of religion, particularly Christianity, but they may not be atheist. Again, people may be atheist but not embrace humanist values; instead they may take a more political position. It is relevant to note that the source of most conflict in the world is religious intolerance.

We think it is important that facilitators present these ideas alongside those of the major world religions, in order to demonstrate that religious belief is both personal and political.

Minority religions

We have also included an overview of primal indigenous, traditional and minority religions in this section because, globally, they still exert a significant influence on people's lives. This is either through their continued practice and/or in the way certain parts have been integrated into more dominant religions. For example, with China set to become a major economic power it seems important to be aware of the continued influence of traditional religion in that part of the world.

Please note: It is not possible here to give a detailed overview of the complex and sophisticated belief systems, death rituals and funeral customs that have evolved in traditional, indigenous and minority religions throughout the world. Some students may wish to do an Internet search extension activity to find out more about these religions. There are numerous websites devoted to this subject.

World Religions (cont.)

Make the session meaningful for your situation

Session 6 will need to be adapted according to the religious, cultural and ethnic make-up of the school. Careful consideration needs to be given to the relative emphasis you place on one religion or another. The session presents an ideal starting point for further work on cultural diversity and the chance to promote a more tolerant and knowledgeable approach to understanding differences in culture and lifestyle.

Be clear about what is being learned

Facilitators should use this material as a tool for promoting tolerance and understanding. We recommend it is presented in a way that is discussion-led and open-minded in order to avoid bias and to model respect for difference. Teachers who have a strong unquestioning belief system must be cautious about the way they present this material. Remember, the 'hidden learning' in your classroom is often as significant as what is officially being learned.

Spread the Word – Christianity

Facts and figures

Christianity is the religion with the largest following in the world. As much as a third of the world's population is Christian and there are an estimated 2 billion followers worldwide, with at least 50 different denominations and many smaller sects.

Christianity originates from the life of Jesus of Nazareth, a Jew, who was born around 4BCE. Jesus, along with some of his twelve disciples, were the main teachers of Christianity.

All Christians believe that there is just one God and that Jesus Christ was the Son of God. They also believe that he died and then rose from the dead three days later. At the heart of Christian belief is the idea of salvation and that Jesus Christ (the Saviour) is still alive in the hearts and actions of his followers.

The Christian Holy Book is known as The Bible. This is divided into the Old Testament (before Jesus was born) and The New Testament (after he was born).

Christians vary in the way they worship and in the emphasis they place on different bits of the bible. Also, like Buddhism, as Christianity has spread, it has often been incorporated with other older religions and cultural practices.

Most Christians worship in a church and a religious leader is known as a Vicar, a Priest, or occasionally a Rector. A bigger and more important place of worship is known as a Cathedral where a Bishop will be in charge of worship. Some Christian sects do not have priests but may have 'elders' and may worship in 'meeting rooms' or a chapel.

Afterlife beliefs

Christians all believe in life after death, and the idea of 'resurrection from the dead' but the details of what actually happens varies according to their denomination. Some Christians do not place much emphasis on life after death, believing that what we do during our lives is more important. For other Christians, the focus of their worship may be preparing for 'Judgement Day'.

Christians believe that the soul goes on after life. If the person lived a good life and believed in God, their soul will go to heaven. If they lived a bad life then their soul will go to hell.

Some Christians picture heaven as a beautiful place of light and peace, in the sky. Here good souls live in harmony with the angels and saints. Hell is sometimes imagined as a fire filled place of endless suffering.

Spread the Word – Christianity (cont.)

For Catholic Christians there is a half-way place called purgatory, where the soul stays for a while to make up for the bad things done in life; later it can go to heaven. Other Christians believe that the soul stays in our bodies when we die and that they will come to life on the Day of Judgement. This is the day when God will end the world and judge everyone, dead or living. These Christians would be buried rather than cremated.

Death rituals and funeral customs

Death rituals and funeral customs vary widely according to denomination and culture.

At the moment of death, if possible, it is usual for members of the family to try to be with their loved one. Catholics, just before death, are given 'extreme unction' and they will be anointed with oil by a priest while the 'last rites' are said.

When someone dies, the funeral usually takes place within a week. This allows time for the body to be washed and laid out by the undertakers for the family to see. The family will also use this time to organise the funeral.

In Ireland, the night before the funeral, a wake will sometimes be held. The body (dressed in ordinary clothes or a simple gown) will be laid in the coffin with the lid open, in the house of the dead person's family. Family and friends will sit around the coffin talking and praying and sometimes singing and remembering too.

On the day of the funeral, the coffin will be carried into the church by family members or the undertakers. A special funeral service will be held. This usually follows written guidelines and will include hymns, prayers and readings from the Bible. It also often includes a special service called Holy Communion, Eucharist or Mass which recalls the 'Last Supper' that Jesus Christ shared with his disciples before his death. At most Christian funerals the coffin lid will be closed but Greek orthodox ceremonies may include an open casket and mourners may bow and then kiss an icon or cross placed on the chest of the deceased. After the funeral, the coffin will be either cremated or buried according to the beliefs of the deceased and their family.

It is traditional to wear black at a Christian funeral and mourning is encouraged. Flowers, sometimes made into wreaths or Christian symbols, may be carried on the coffin or beside it and placed on the grave.

Burial is usually in a graveyard beside the church. A tombstone will be inscribed with the dates the person lived and perhaps an epitaph. After cremation, the family may choose a plot with a small headstone. Alternatively, they may do something more personal like scatter the ashes or bury them and then plant a tree in memory of the person.

Spread the Word – Christianity (cont.)

In the West, a small private funeral is sometimes followed by a memorial service at a later date. This allows family and friends to celebrate the life of the deceased and will not necessarily be a religious event.

Families often visit and tend the grave. Sometimes this will be each week when they go to church on Sunday. More often it will be on anniversaries such as the birthday of, or date on which, the person died.

This verse from the New Testament sums up the Christian view of death as the beginning of life with God.

'O death where is thy sting?

O grave where is thy victory?'

(Corinthians I 1.55)

Spread the Word – Islam

Facts and figures

Islam has about 1.3 billion followers worldwide who are known as Muslims. After Christianity it is the second most influential religion in the world with about a quarter of the world's population now Muslim. It is also the fastest growing religion.

There are two main groups of Muslims; Sunni and Shi'ah. These two groups have developed because of a dispute over who should lead Islam after the death of Muhammed.

Islam means 'submission' (or submit to God). It is a monotheistic religion as well as a way of life. It originated through the life and work of Muhammad who was born in 570 CE. Muslims believe that Allah chose Muhammed to carry his message to the world. It was given to him by an angel and is written down as the Qur'an. The Qur'an explains that the original message of Judaism and Christianity, as given by the Bible prophets, has been corrupted. As such it is not a new religion, but a 'final call' to return to a purer, more authentic religion and lifestyle.

As well as the Qur'an, Muslims have a second holy book called the Hadith which is a collection of writings and sayings of Muhammed and his followers.

Muslims worship in a mosque where the officiating priest is known as an Imam. A mullah (or religious scholar and teacher) is another important member of a mosque.

The five pillars of Islam are religious duties that every Muslim must do. Shahadah (worship), Salah (prayers), Zakah (giving to charity), Sawn (fasting during Ramadan), and Hajj (pilgrimage to Makkah).

Afterlife beliefs

Muslims believe in life after death. They believe that the 'angel of death' takes the soul to Barzakh. This is a special place where time does not exist and where souls wait for the 'Day of Judgement'.

The Day of Judgement is the end of the world. Earth will be destroyed and Allah (God) will come to judge the dead and the living. Those who have lived good lives will go to Paradise and those who have lived bad lives go to hell where they live in fire and suffer forever. In the Qur'an, Paradise is described as a beautiful garden to which an angel leads you through an emerald gate. In this garden rocks and pebbles are made of jewels and gold and even the soil smells sweet like perfume. It is never too hot or too cold and there are flowers which bloom and birds singing.

Muslims believe that on the Day of Judgement we will have our bodies restored; as such cremation is forbidden.

Spread the Word – Islam (cont.)

Death rituals and funeral customs

If possible the moment of death is spent with family and friends who will read from the Qur'an, particularly from Surah (chapter) 97, which answers basic questions about life after death and Judgement Day. If the dying person is able, they should say the Ash-Shahada: 'There is no God but Allah and Muhammed is the Prophet of Allah.' After death, the person must be buried as soon as possible. The body will be washed three times with soap, starting with the ears, nose, mouth, head, feet, hands and forearms (as before prayer). The body will then be anointed with perfume and wrapped in three pieces of white cotton called a kafan.

At the mosque the coffin lies in front of the Imam who will face Makkah and together with the congregation they will say the funeral prayer – the Salat ul-Janazah. This has within it prayers which ask Allah for mercy and forgiveness for the dead person. Unlike normal prayer times the congregation remain standing throughout.

The burial takes place in a Muslim Cemetry or part of one assigned to Muslims. Muslims are always buried with their head facing towards the holy city of Makkah. It is customary for their head to be turning towards the right and traditionally a coffin is not used (unless a law stipulates their use). Funerals are simple and respectful ceremonies. Mourners may throw a handful of earth onto the coffin or shroud wrapped body. The grave will be a raised mound of earth, marked with a simple stone; large monuments are discouraged.

Families typically mourn for a period of three days and it is common to read the Qur'an at this time as a source of comfort. A special meal may also be shared to remember the deceased.

The grave is then visited each Friday for 40 days and usually no weddings or other celebrations will be held for three months.

When people hear of the death of someone they may say a common saying, which sums up one of the basic ideas of Islam:

'To God we belong and to him we return.'

S6 Spread the Word – Hinduism

Facts and figures

There are an estimated 900 million Hindus in the world. This is about 15% of the world's population. Hinduism originated in India where most of its followers still live. Many Hindus believe their religion has been around forever. Modern Hinduism can be traced back to about 1750BCE but there are now many different traditions and sects. Like all religions, Hinduism has adapted and changed as its followers live in other countries; nonetheless great importance is still placed on the sacred places of India such as the River Ganges.

Hinduism is a pantheistic religion, which means that Hindus believe that God can be seen everywhere and in all things. There are thousands of Gods in Hinduism but they are, in fact, all manifestations or ways of understanding the one 'God' (or divine presence) Brahman. Central to Hinduism is a belief in reincarnation and the caste system which explains why people have different roles. The caste you are born into depends on your previous life. If you led a good life you will be rewarded by being born into a higher caste.

Hindus believe that cows should not be killed and that they are symbolic of the sanctity of life. Many Hindus are also vegetarian.

There are numerous sacred texts and commentaries in Hinduism. The best known and most important is the Bhagavad Gita (written in about 300 BCE) which, through Krishna, gives access to the divine to ordinary people. There are also the more ancient Vedas, revered by all branches of Hinduism, and written in 1000-1500 BCE by the mythical founders of Hinduism who 'heard' them during meditation.

Hindus worship in a temple and a priest will officiate over ceremonies. Religious teachers and wise men are known as Gurus. Gurus often set up their own branch of Hinduism and followers may attend an Ashram for worship and study with their Guru.

Afterlife beliefs

Hindus believe in reincarnation. They believe that most people are reborn after death in a new body. The soul, or atman, does not change but the body does. We are given a new life and body as a reward or punishment for the kind of life lived previously. We go through many rebirths and the purpose of religion is to help us lead a better life each time so that eventually we do not have to come back. If you lead an exceptionally good life you may break out of this cycle of dying and being reborn. This cycle is called Samsara and the act of breaking free is called Moksha, which means you can go to join Brahma (the supreme God).

Hindus believe in other sort of half-way heavens where the various Gods and Goddesses live. These are places where your soul can rest in between lives on earth.

Spread the Word – Hinduism (cont.)

Death rituals and funeral customs

Ideally a Hindu will die while lying on the floor in contact with the earth. Touching the corpse is seen as polluting but it is done in order to say farewell and as such part of the mourning ritual is a cleansing act.

During life there are sixteen samskaras (special ceremonies) which guide us along the path of self-improvement. The final one of these is cremation. Hindus believe that it is the soul, not the body, which is needed after we die. The physical body is thought to be made of fire, air, earth and water. Cremation brings the body back to fire and air, the ashes are earth and these will be scattered on water. A Hindu funeral is both a celebration and a remembrance service.

Traditionally, the body is cremated within 24 hours. The dead body will be wrapped in a shroud of new cloth and a piece of gold or silver will be placed in the mouth and sometimes on the eyes as well. A last (symbolic) food offering will be made to the deceased before cremation. In India the flower covered coffin will be burnt on a funeral pyre (a big bonfire), using ghee (a kind of butter) to help the flames. In Britain the ceremony takes place in a crematorium. White is the traditional colour of mourning and traditional garments will be worn. A noise is often made as the funeral procession makes its way to the crematorium or pyre; horns and bells may be used. The chief mourner (traditionally the eldest son) will stand near the coffin and ignite the pyre. In a crematorium he will usually push the button to close the curtains around the coffin, as well as ignite the cremator. Sometimes the male mourners will shave their heads as a sign of bereavement. As the body burns, prayers and readings from the Bhagavad Gita or other Hindu scriptures will be read. Three days later, the ashes will be collected and if possible they will be scattered on the Ganges River. Hindus sometimes describe our soul's journey as like a river travelling towards the sea which is why they scatter the ashes onto running water.

Finally, ten or twelve days after the cremation the kriya/shraddha ceremony is held. Pinda (rice balls) will be made and offered by the eldest son followed by rice cooked in milk. These are offered to all deceased relatives and ancestors, not just the relative who has just died.

Between the time of the death and the kriya it is expected that normal life stops. The role of friends and family is vital at this time as they will bring gifts and food. The family are considered unclean until the final act of the sixteenth samskara takes place. It is believed that the soul has now been reborn and the old person no longer exists in any form. After the thirteenth day, public mourning can now cease and a large feast will be held. The deceased will then be remembered in daily worship (Puja).

S6 Spread the Word – Hinduism (cont.)

'For to one that is born, death is certain: and to one that dies, birth is certain. Therefore do not grieve over what is unavoidable.'

A Hindu Prayer

'From the unreal lead me to the real

From darkness lead me to light

From death lead me to immortality.'

The Brihad-Aranyaka (Unpanishad)

Spread the Word – Buddhism

Facts and figures

There are thought to be about 360 million Buddhists in the world. This includes more than five hundred varieties of Buddhism, which highlights the way it adapts itself to suit lifestyle and culture. Central to all varieties of Buddhism is the belief that we should pursue wisdom through meditation. Buddhists may worship in a temple or more simply in an 'ashram' which is a place of retreat for meditation. Buddhism has many ordained monks and nuns who follow a religious life. Becoming a Buddhist means committing to what is known as 'The Three Jewels'; the Buddha (being awake), Dharma (tools for transformation) and Sangha (the Buddhist community).

Buddhists follow the teachings of Buddha (literally the 'enlightened one') who lived in India about 2,500 years ago. The Buddha believed that the cause of all human unhappiness and discontent is our 'craving' for more and our clinging or attachment to what is essentially 'unreal'. Buddhists also follow the teachings of other 'Buddhas' and teachers of Buddhism, and everyone is encouraged to 'find their own path' to enlightenment.

Buddhists believe that everything is impermanent and that through meditation we become 'awake' to this reality and then we are more able to just enjoy what we have rather than to always be looking for something else. Buddhists do not believe in a creator or 'all-seeing, all-knowing' judging God. They believe we all have divine potential. The most important Buddhist scriptures are the Sutras which are the collected sayings of the Buddha and the Pali Canon which includes stories about the Buddha's life, plus guidance on meditation. Another important book is the Tibetan Book of the Dead which gives detailed advice on the moment of death and the journey to our next life.

Afterlife beliefs

Most types of Buddism believe in reincarnation but they do not believe we have individual souls separate from our bodies. Instead, each person is made up from five interrelated parts – body, feelings, perceptions, will and consciousness. These can be taken apart and put back together in many different ways. This and karma determine what your next life will be like. You are born and die many times. Buddhists believe that the cycle of life goes around and around like a wheel until we break free and reach Nirvana.

Some Buddhists also believe in different heavens where past and future Buddhas live, and where you can rest in between your births on earth. One of the most important is Tushita heaven where Maitreya, the Buddha to come, lives. He will come to earth in 30,000 years to remind us of how we should live.

S6 Spread the Word – Buddhism (cont.)

Death rituals and funeral customs

There is a wide variety in Buddhist belief and practice around death. Some Japanese Buddhist ceremonies are similar to Christian ceremonies in the West with a eulogy and prayers.

Other traditions have several separate ceremonies, held over days and weeks. Typically these culminate in a ceremony in which a meditation is made on behalf of the deceased to help them in their new incarnation.

Buddhists place great emphasis on the person's state of mind leading up to death. There are special meditations which can be used by the dying person and/or friends and families. Typically, when someone is dying, there will be readings from the sutras (the collected sayings of the Buddha).

There are few formal traditions relating to Buddhist funerals because they are not really viewed as religious events. The coffin may be decorated with flowers and gifts (which will be passed on to the monks after the service) and a simple ceremony with prayers will be held. Traditionally the coffin will be open and the guests are expected to see the body as a valuable reminder of the impermanence of everything.

Alternatively, a photograph may be used as a symbolic reminder of impermanence.

Public grief and mourning is not a feature of Buddhist bereavement because they believe death brings us closer to God. White is often worn at funerals and the emphasis is on acceptance of loss rather than grieving the loss.

Most Buddhists will be cremated and a simple ceremony will be held where Buddhist and other readings may be read. Many Buddists share the Tibetan belief that after 49 days the soul is reborn into its next life. At this point special prayers and meditation techniques may be used to aid the person on their journey to the next life.

'There is an island, an island which you cannot go beyond. It is a place of nothingness, a place of no possessions and attachments. It is the total end of death and decay and this is why I call it Nirvana, the extinguished, the cool.'

Spread the Word – Sikhism

Facts and figures

Sikhism was started in India about 500 years ago by a holy man called Guru Nanak, and there are now an estimated 23 million Sikhs worldwide. It has its origins in traditional Hinduism but there are many differences. Guru Nanak taught a new way of thinking which emphasises dealing with the realities of life as well as tolerance and equality for all. In Sikhism right conduct and truth are closely linked. A person cannot be said to know the truth or be close to God unless it is shown in their behaviour. Sikhs believe there is one God and worship in a temple known as a gurdwara.

Sikhism teaches that God (Waheguru) has spoken to humans through ten great teachers or Gurus.

Their Holy Book, the Guru Granth Sahib, has replaced human Gurus and is considered to be the last and eternal Guru. The Guru Granth Sahib is not worshipped but it will be given a place of honour in the temple and when Sikhs enter the temple they show their respect for the book by taking off their shoes and covering their heads.

Instructions for religious ceremonies are set out in another important book called the Sikh Rahit Marjada. Sikhism has five symbols known as the 5 K's (bracelet, long hair, comb, kirpan-sword and shorts).

Sikhism is a religion of tolerance. It is not as strict as some religions and open to the idea of adapting to the culture in which we live.

Afterlife beliefs

Sikhs believe in reincarnation and that our souls are separate from our bodies. When we die, Sikhs believe that the soul leaves the body and is reborn. Death is like a long sleep before being reborn. Sikhs believe that being born a human means we are part way to returning to God but we may have to go through many rebirths before reaching God. During life on earth, Sikhs aim to be mindful of death so that the cycle of rebirth is broken and we may return to God. Learning to focus our attention on God rather than ourselves is called mukti (or salvation) and means we can be freed from the cycle of life and death.

Death rituals and funeral customs

'Because the soul never dies, there is no mourning at the death of a Sikh.'

Family and friends will gather around the dying person to read the Hymn of Peace – the Sukhmani written by Guru Arjan. The dying person will try to say 'Waheguru' (wonderful God) just before they die. Death is welcomed in Sikhism because it brings

Spread the Word – Sikhism (cont.)

them closer to God. The focus of the ceremonial prayers will be on releasing the soul from the bonds of reincarnation. Mourning is seen as symbolising a desire to be separate from God. It is not encouraged because it goes against the hopes and beliefs of Sikhism.

Traditionally, Sikhs prepare the body for the funeral with a yogurt bath while reciting prayers. Next, the body will be dressed in new clothes, and with the five symbols of Sikhism, placed in a coffin. Prayers will be said and the coffin will then be taken to the gurdwara, but it will not be taken inside. In the West it will be taken to a crematorium but in India it may be burned on an outdoor pyre. It is usual for just the men of the family to attend the cremation. Following a prayer for peace for the soul, the Sohila (an evening or bedtime prayer) will be said. Family and friends will then return to the gurdwara where a speech about the dead person will be made. This will be followed by saying Sukhmans which are psalms and songs of peace from the holy book. The service then ends with the sharing of karah parshad (special food). As for most Sikh ceremonies it is common for there to be a feast in the langar (free kitchen) and for gifts to be given to the poor and donations made to the gurdwara itself.

The ashes are typically collected the next day and they are then scattered with flowers on to a running stream or river. For up to ten days after the funeral, the family will take turns to read the entire Siri Guru from cover to cover. The passage describing the death of Guru Amar Da is left to be read on the tenth day. During this period friends and family visit and help the family settle back to normal life.

A later memorial service may be held at the family home.

Sohila – A Sikh prayer

'Know the real reason why you are here.

Collect up your treasure under the Guru's guidance. Make your mind into God's home. If God is with you always, you will not be reborn.'

Spread the Word – Judaism

Facts and figures

There are 14 million followers of Judaism worldwide. Most followers are also Jewish. Judaism is a monotheistic religion. Worship takes place in a synagogue and the religious leader is known as a Rabbi. Like many religions, there is wide variation in both religious practice and belief. This is particularly the case regarding beliefs and practices around death.

The Jewish Holy Books are the Talmud (actually a collection of books and a commentary on the Bible) and the Torah (the Christian 'Old Testament' or 'Jewish' Bible). Together these two books provide guidance for the Jewish people. For Jews what is right and wrong is decided by God's laws, of which there are 613, that God wants us to keep. The great teachers include Talmudic scholars, the Old Testament prophets and Jesus.

The Torah tells the story of the Father of Judaism, Abraham. It is here that the Ten Commandments (rules from God) are also written. Based on what is written in the Torah, Jews believe that they are God's chosen people and that God has promised them the land of Israel.

The history of the Jews is a complicated political story which reached its worst point during the Second World War when 6 million Jews were put to death as part of Hitler's final solution to annihilate the Jewish race and build a new Germany. In 1948, the State of Israel was recognised and Jews began to return to their 'homeland' in the middle-east. Unfortunately, this was also where many Muslims had settled over the centuries and so the land is a source of constant conflict between these two religions.

Afterlife beliefs

Teachings about Heaven and life after death are not emphasised in Judaism. How we live our lives here on earth is considered more important and prayer is seen almost like talking to God in heaven. Even so Jewish people do believe that heaven is God's home and the souls of good people will go there to be with God. Some Jews believe at the moment of death the soul goes immediately to God and stays there watching what is happening on earth. Others say that the souls remain with the dead bodies waiting for the Final Day when the Messiah (a special servant of God) will come to earth. On that day the dead will rise in their bodies from their graves and come to the Messiah. This is known as the resurrection. In the meantime there are rough equivalents to heaven and hell, with righteous souls able to enjoy the pleasures of olam ha'bah, 'the world to come' which has a Garden of Eden like quality; and wicked souls condemned to the fiery pits of Gehenna. Other Jews believe in 'transmigration of souls' which is like

Spread the Word – Judaism (cont.)

reincarnation and means they believe that the soul comes back to earth in a new body. Traditional Jews never burn the bodies at death because they believe we come back at Judgement Day in our bodies.

Death rituals and funeral customs

If possible, the dying person will die with the words of the great prayer, Shema Israel on his or her lips: 'Hear O Israel the Lord our God is one God.'

Jewish funerals are a time for intense public mourning which are governed by a set of rituals and traditions that apply to the seven family members (spouse, mother, father, son, daughter, brother or sister). Rituals vary according to which sect the person belonged to but all Jewish communities will have a Chevra Kadisha, who prepares the body for burial and arrange the funeral. The body should be buried within 24 hours of the death but may be delayed to allow for family who need to travel. The body will be washed, anointed with spices, wrapped in a linen sheet and placed in a plain coffin. The coffin lid will always be kept closed.

At the funeral, the coffin will be taken from the synagogue to a Jewish Cemetery where family and friends will gather in the chapel. A symbolic small tear may be made in the mourner's (usually black) clothes, which represents a broken heart and recalls former days when mourners would rip their garments to express their grief. No flowers are allowed.

A eulogy will be given by the Rabbi or close friend. The Kaddish (a Hebrew prayer) will be said by male relatives both before and after the coffin is interred. Mourners always stand to say the kaddish and face towards Jerusalem, the Jewish Holy City, in Israel. Traditionally, there is a slow procession from the chapel to the grave itself, with several pauses along the way. It is considered an honour to help fill the grave with earth and everyone will join in. This is followed by a symbolic washing of hands and everyone returns home. For the next seven days the family is in full mourning – shiva. Friends look after them by providing food and encouraging them to express their grief. The Kaddish is said every day. After shiva, mourners can return to normal life, but they are forbidden from going to any entertainment or celebration for 30 days. Finally, for a further 11 months, the kaddish must be said every day. A longer period may be needed for people who led 'wicked' lives.

The anniversary of the death is called a yahrzeit, upon which the bereaved will attend a service with prayers, at the synagogue and light a candle at home for 24 hours. Often the unveiling of the headstone will take place at this time and a simple ceremony will be held at the graveside. The grave will be visited at least annually, usually around Jewish

Spread the Word – Judaism (cont.)

new year as well as on the anniversary of the death. This is done to ensure the person is remembered and as a comfort to those left behind.

A Jewish prayer

'O thou who art at home

Deep in my heart

Enable me to join you

Deep in my heart.'

The Talmud

Spread the Word – Indigenous, Traditional and Other Minority Religions

Facts and figures

It is hard to give accurate figures but over the last century there has been a significant decline in worldwide numbers of people following indigenous, traditional and minority religions. This decline is due to a number of factors including the suppression of religion under communism, European colonialism and the influence of Western capitalism. In many cultures minority religious practice continued throughout this period, without the official authorities knowing. Also, elements of these religions may have survived or been adapted to the demands of modern life, or the more dominant belief system – particularly Christianity.

As many as 150 million people practice what can be called primal indigenous religions. A further 225 million people practice Chinese Traditional Religion. Similarly, although participation in traditional African religion has declined from 60% to 11% over the last century, worldwide there are an estimated 95 million followers of African traditional and diasporic religions.

For example, Rastafarianism (started in the 1930s) combines Christianity with African traditions alongside a more political or 'nationalist' belief in returning to the homeland of Ethiopia.

Similarly, Chinese traditional religions, Taoism and Confucianism, are often combined together with aspects of Buddhism. Although suppressed under Communism (where atheism was the official state religion) for much of the 20th Century it is estimated that the majority of rural Chinese people still practise aspects of these religions, particularly with regard to beliefs and customs around death.

Native American, South-east Asian and Aboriginal religions are three indigenous religions, that continue to exert a significant influence within minority communities in America, Polynesia and Australia.

Indigenous religions share certain characteristics. For example, there are often male shamans (priests) or medicine men who can link the spirit world with the physical world. The use of hallucinogenic plants to aid ritual, ceremony and meditation is another feature common to these religions.

These religions often share a deep respect for the natural world of animals and plants, and a way of life that is either nomadic or based on hunting.

They are often pantheistic, meaning they believe that the divine is to be experienced everywhere. Alternatively, they may be polytheistic and have many Gods. Indigenous

Spread the Word – Indigenous, Traditional and Other Minority Religions (cont.)

religion often moves in rhythm with the seasons and may imbue the geographical world of mountains and rivers with supernatural properties. Some of these religions also have a good understanding of astronomy and religious leaders will often have skills in the use of traditional herbs and medicines.

There are a number of 'modern' minority religions such as the Mormons, Unitarian and Baha'I faith, which all began within the last 150 years. The Baha'I and Unitarian faith both embrace humanist principles and emphasise the need for religions to work together to create a world based on peace, justice and equality and to end prejudice and intolerance.

Since the late 20th Century, in Europe and North America, there has been a growth of interest in 'new age' religions and spiritual eclecticism. This includes Gaia theory and the revival of Wicca and 'earth-centred' belief systems. Followers tend to use a mix of pagan, shamanistic and complementary medicines combined with humanist and 'alternative' lifestyle choices to arrive at an individual and 'holistic' approach to life and death.

Finally, mention needs to be made of the influence of Zoroaistrinism established by Zarathushtra between 1000 and 1500 BCE in Iran or what was Persia. It is thought to be the first monotheistic religion and has about 140,000 followers today. Its followers were persecuted and fled to northern India in the 7th Century where they remain settled as the Parse community. Significant to their death rituals is the practice of leaving the dead on a high tower for the vultures to eat. This practice demonstrates commitment to a belief that life is something that should be dedicated to a greater good.

Afterlife

Beliefs in the afterlife vary widely. They often include joining ancestors and a return to 'the source' (earth or spirit) depending on creation myths while some believe that we take our bodies into the next life.

Death rituals and funeral customs

Again these will vary widely according to the religion and culture.

It is not possible here to give a detailed overview of the complex and sophisticated belief systems, death rituals and funeral customs that evolved in traditional, indigenous and minority religions throughout the world. Some students may wish to do an Internet search extension activity to find out more about these religions.

S6 Spread the Word – Indigenous, Traditional and Other Minority Religions (cont.)

'My daily life is dedicated to serving the kami (spirits) with a true heart. The kami are our ancestors and we must pray to them with respect and sincerity. This is the way to heaven.'

A Shinto priest

'We are all visitors to this time, this place. We are just passing through. Our purpose here is to observe, to learn, to grow, to love...and then we return home.'

Aboriginal proverb

World Religions

Use one of the handouts on world religions to help you answer these questions.

Religion ....

Approximate numbers worldwide ....

Great teachers ....

Holy book(s) ....

Place of worship ....

Religious leader ....

Beliefs about the afterlife ....

....

Customs at the moment of death ....

....

Laying out of the body and viewing of the body ....

....

Funeral rituals ....

....

Burial or cremation ....

Grieving process and mourning rituals ....

....

Similarities with other religions ....

....

Differences (is there anything that is unique to this religion?) ....

....

Anything else? ....

Beliefs and Customs of the World Religions

Religion / Belief	Christianity	Islam	Hinduism	Buddhism	Sikhism	Judaism	Minority religions
Numbers							
Teachers							
Holy books							
Place of worship							
Afterlife beliefs							
Death rituals							
Burial or cremation							
Funeral customs							
Anything else?							

Burial or Cremation?

Discuss and then list the advantages and disadvantages:

Burial

Advantages

....
....
....
....
....

Disadvantages

....
....
....
....
....

Cremation

Advantages

....
....
....
....
....

Disadvantages

....
....
....
....
....

Session 7
Feelings and Thoughts

Introduction

In this session, students are asked to focus more upon themselves and their personal responses to death and loss. They are asked to identify personal experiences and feelings and to also consider and perhaps confront some of their own fears and concerns. The activities therefore need to be introduced and delivered with particular care and sensitivity and the facilitator may need to forewarn some students prior to the start of the session.

Talk time

The group should be reminded of the ground rules at the start of this session. This will help make the group feel safer and encourage appropriate levels of self-disclosure.

Introduce today's topic by using the Circle Time tool 'silent statements' which allow pupils to share information without speaking. Prepare an opening statement as follows:

'Today's talk time is a bit different because we will not be talking, we will be making 'silent statements'. We will be communicating and sharing but you do not have to speak. I will say something, for example, 'I like chocolate.' If it's true for you then raise your hand. There is no talking but I'd like you to look around the group and notice who has raised their hand and who hasn't. If you are the only person who has raised their hand, that's fine. Remember we said we will... (quote ground rules). If it's true for you but you don't want to join in, then don't raise your hand. Please remember also that we speak only for ourselves.'

It will help if you practise this with a few ready prepared 'low risk' statements such as, 'I have got a bike,' or, 'I have been to London'. It's important that this activity is done in silence.

Choose a selection from the following statements. They are written to move from low risk to high risk and back to low risk. Join in this activity yourself and add statements more suitable to your group.

- I've had a pet that died.
- I've visited someone in hospital.
- I've seen and heard an ambulance with its siren on.
- I've spent time in hospital myself.
- I've seen someone die on TV.
- I nearly died once.
- I thought I was going to die once.
- I helped save someone's life.
- I've killed someone or something in a computer game.
- I know what a funeral is like.
- I've been to a funeral.
- I know someone who has died.
- Someone I know committed suicide.
- Someone close to me in my family has died.

- I've seen someone die.
- I know someone who is very ill and who may be dying.
- I'm worried about someone I know dying.
- I think about death a bit/a lot/never.
- I'm scared of dying.
- I believe in life after death.
- I would like to be cremated not buried.

Thank the students for taking part in this activity and summarise some facts and figures about the group. (The co-facilitator may take notes during this activity.)

For example:

- Two people have had someone in their family die.
- Everyone has seen a death on TV.
- Most of us have personal experience of loss but not all of death.
- We need to be sensitive to those people.

Activity 1 – Feelings

Students can brainstorm the following question: 'What feelings do we associate with death?'

The facilitator can use a flip-chart to make a written record of students' ideas. Alternatively, use the worksheet 'What Feelings Do We Associate with Death?' as a way of recording small group or individual brainstorms. As in Session 1 Activity 3, 'Feelings Associated with Loss?' it is hoped that this activity will both consolidate and extend student's emotional vocabulary. Similarly, it should raise awareness of the vocabulary that exists to describe the wide continuum of deaths that we experience.

Activity 2 – A questionnaire

Students can now work individually on the questionnaire 'Feelings and Thoughts About Death'. This sheet prompts them to reflect on their own ideas and feelings about death and to consider the kind of death they would choose if that was possible. It also, in part, mirrors some of the content of talk time thereby reinforcing that work and provide a written record.

A variation on this could be for students to work in pairs and interview each other. Alternatively it could be done using a tape-recorder.

Activity 3 - My Life Journey

Students can be asked to illustrate their own life journey. It would be helpful for the facilitator to prompt thinking by writing up a series of questions on the flip-chart as follows:

- How long would you like to live?
- What would you like to do in your life along this journey?
- Who would you like to meet?
- What job would you like to have?
- Who would you like to love?
- Where would you like to visit and go?
- What will you do in order to ensure your life expectancy is not shortened, e.g. exercise, looking after your health, etc.
- How would you choose to die?

Plenary

Students can brainstorm the following questions:

- How did we feel and think about death at the start of this session?
- How do we now feel and think about death?

The facilitator can record students' responses on the flip-chart and highlight any similarities and differences.

What Feelings Do You Associate with Death?

Feelings and Thoughts About Death

Have you ever experienced the death of someone close to you – if so who?

....

....

Whose death do you most fear – why is this?

....

....

Do you ever think about your own death and how do you feel about this?

....

....

Have you ever been to a funeral – what was it like?

....

....

Do you believe in life after death? If so, what are your reasons for this?

....

....

Does religion play any part in your attitude towards death?

....

....

What would be your best and worst kind of death to experience?

....

....

Is there anything else you feel or think about the subject of death?

....

....

....

....

Session 8
Questions and Answers

Introduction

In this session the students are encouraged to discuss more complex questions relating to controversial subjects such as suicide, murder, hit and run accidents, drugs, war, mass tragedies, assisted death, medical intervention, terminal illness, life-support, abortion and so on. The facilitator's key role here is to encourage discussion and not to provide answers or give your own opinions.

It may be helpful to refer to Session 4, Activity 3 'Any Questions?' and for the facilitator to thus be prepared to give some factual information regarding students' questions.

The introduction will need to be prepared carefully and tailored to the group. The facilitator may like to use a poem or reading (for example *Lady Lazarus* in *The Collected Poems of Sylvia Plath*) as an introduction to the session and as a prompt for talk time.

Talk time

The students can focus on the following questions:

- What do we know about suicide?
- Why do we think people commit suicide?
- Do we think that suicide is a sin as it is a deliberate destruction of a gift from God'?
- Do we believe that it is a human right for everyone to terminate his or her own life if they so choose?

It may be useful for one of the facilitators to scribe here in order to record students' views. It is important that the facilitators avoid providing answers or giving their own personal views. Rather they should aim to summarise the discussion and ensure that the group rules are adhered to. This subject may evoke strong responses and the faciltitator's role is to ensure that tolerance is modelled and different beliefs are respected.

Activity 1 – Cry for help (bullying and suicide)

Students can be handed the case study, which details one student's experiences of bullying which ultimately led to their suicide. They can then focus on the question, 'What are the Feelings Associated with Suicide?'. When considering this question it will be important to focus on not only the feelings of the person who committed suicide but also on the feelings that this act may have created in others, e.g. family friends, peers, the bullies etc. The students could focus on the kinds of words and images that the word itself generates both for them and for those in their group.

Activity 2 – What's your opinion...?

Distribute the cards 'What's Your Opinion...?'. Each card asks a question which demands a reflective and ethical response. The students can be divided into groups and asked to work through the cards and discuss them. If there is time, ask students to feed back to the whole group. Summarise their discussions in terms of a few key points, which should include:

- These are complex questions which require considered and sometimes complex solutions.
- There is rarely a open and shut case for or against in these situations.
- Some religions make it seem as if there is a simple solution to some of these questions. Maybe it's easier to have a higher authority make decisions for us than having to take responsibility for our own choices.

Activity 3 – Role-play

Divide the group into groups of three and use the scenario cards 'Questions and Answers?' as the basis for role-plays. Each student can be allocated a role: character A, character B or that of an observer.

For each scenario the facilitator will need to make sure that adequate preparation time is given. (What led up to this situation? How old are you? What's your story etc?) Once students have completed their role-play, they may wish to discuss how it 'felt' to participate, to 'be' character A or B and to be the observer.

Plenary

In this session, students will have focused upon some controversial and often very difficult issues. They will not have been provided with a set of answers or solutions – because these do not exist. However, it is important that they are given the opportunity to become more aware of these complex questions and the kinds of responses that they (and others) may and do have towards them.

It may be helpful for the facilitator to use some of these key questions:

- What do we think, feel and believe about suicide?
- When is death more or less significant and complex?
- Is there a right or wrong way to die?
- Is there such a thing as a 'bad' death?
- Who or what can help when someone has died in a distressing way?

Follow-on activities

- Students can investigate the range of organisations and groups who support families when a suicide has occurred.
- It may be helpful to arrange for an outside speaker to discuss their work with the group, e.g. the Samaritans or the Shadow of Suicide Group or the Compassionate Friends Group.
- Students can collect stories and examples from newspapers, i.e. switching off life support machines, abortions, a woman's right to choose, etc. and then use these as prompts for debate or discussion.
- It may be useful to invite someone from a local funeral directors or a humanist organisation to talk with the students about death customs. It will be helpful for the students to identify the questions they would like answered prior to the visit.
- Students can focus upon terminal illness as most of the group will have some knowledge or experience of cancer, for example. It may be helpful to contact Cancer Research in order to investigate not only statistics and facts about the disease but to also find out about how people are emotionally and psychologically supported throughout the process of dying in this way.

Cry for Help – Jason's Suicide

Case study

Jason was 15 when the bullying began. He had just started a new school. Everyone's first day at school is traumatic but his was probably worse than most. He didn't look any different from the other kids but as soon as he arrived at school, everyone stared at him. Then, at lunchtime, the bullying began. A group of other students surrounded him and started to call him 'gypo'. Some of them even spat at him. Jason couldn't understand this – it was like they hadn't even got to know him - yet they decided they didn't like him just because he didn't live in a house like them. His family were Irish travellers, which meant that they lived in caravans and moved around from field to field with about 100 other relatives. He had already lived in 20 different places and he loved his way of life – it felt free – but other people obviously had a big problem with it. Instead of looking at him as a normal teenager, they had always assumed that he was a criminal. That's why he got picked on at school. Every day he was told again and again to 'go back to Ireland'. At break times he would stand scared and motionless while people taunted him. He couldn't understand why people should hate him so much. He'd done nothing to hurt them, he'd not tried to abuse them or threaten them.

Finally, one of the other boys at school attacked him. He was sat down having lunch when a boy came up to him and said he wanted to fight a gypsy. Then he punched him. Jason was so shocked – he attempted to defend himself but the other boy carried on pulling his hair and lunging into his face until a teacher separated them. After that, the thought of going into school made him feel physically sick. He had no friends there. He felt unhappy and withdrawn. He wasn't the carefree kind of person that he used to be. His mum didn't mind him not going into school – she was quite cool with him. But the problem was that the depression had set in. He stayed at home with his six brothers and sisters where he felt safe but he also felt sad, withdrawn and more and more depressed as every day wore on.

Then one day, when he was returning from a trip to the shops, two of the boys who had bullied him in school followed him. They beat him up really badly. They broke his nose, they broke his arm and fractured his left leg. He had to go to hospital and stayed in there for two weeks. By this time he could barely talk to anybody. One night on the ward he decided that he just couldn't face going home. He didn't feel safe outside of the hospital on the streets or in school. He got hold of some tablets. He didn't even stop to think – he just wanted some release from all the pain and the agony that he felt he had been suffering for so long. He took the tablets. He died. Did anyone care?

What's Your Opinion...?

People who are terminally ill and in a lot of pain should be allowed to be helped to die in a dignified way.

Women should be allowed to have an abortion on demand.

If someone commits suicide they will go to hell.

Capital punishment should be allowed for some crimes.

Parents should be allowed to let very disabled children die if they choose.

Refugees have probably lost more than they will ever gain by moving to England.

What's Your Opinion...? (cont.)

I would not want to be kept alive on a life-support machine if I was in a coma.

People who self-harm are just trying to get attention.

Eating disorders and being obsessed with what your body looks like is on the increase amongst both boys and girls. Why do you think this is?

Hit and run drivers who kill someone should be banned from driving for life.

If someone really wants to kill themselves they will. There's nothing you can do.

People with AIDS should not be allowed to be teachers.

What's Your Opinion...? (cont.)

It's worse if your mum dies than your dad.

There is always a good reason for bad behaviour. Do you think this applies to pupils who get excluded?

People who end up homeless are losers.

Questions and Answers – Role-play Scenarios

In threes, with one person being the observer, role-play one or more of the following scenarios. Take turns to be A, B or observer.

Person A is about to jump off a bridge. His partner has just left him.

Person B is a stranger who tries to stop him.

Person A is feeling suicidal and phones the Samaritans.

Person B is a volunteer Samaritan working a nightshift on the telephone helpline.

Person A is the mother who is 60 with a very painful and terminal illness. She has been given three months to live and she begs **Person B**, her son, to help her to end her life by taking an extra dose of the prescribed drug.

Person A is a 16 year old young woman who is pregnant. Her boyfriend, **Person B**, is also 16. She wants to have an abortion, he wants to keep the baby.

For each one, make sure you allow time to prepare (what led up to this situation, how old are you? What's your story etc.?) and complete the role-play, and for students to feed back to each other how it felt doing the role-play.

Session 9
The Grief Cycle

Introduction

This topic can be introduced to the group via the illustration on the sheet 'The Grief Cycle'. This illustrates the stages that a bereaved person will usually go through when a loved one dies.

The facilitator should point out that grief is a normal and essential response to the death of someone that we love. This process can be short term or long term depending upon the people involved and the type of relationship. It is usually the case that the death of a wife, husband, parent or child would tend to be the most difficult to cope with and will generally result in a longer grieving process. The facilitator may wish to outline the stages of grief as follows:

Shock and disbelief

This occurs in response to the death at the outset and it can take the form of very real physical pain or even numbness. For some people this kind of shock displays itself in apathy and withdrawal which can act as some kind of defence mechanism allowing the individual to cope with their so-called normal life. A person in shock may say, 'I can't believe it!'

Denial

The denial stage usually occurs within the first couple of weeks and can last from a very short period of time to many weeks. The bereaved person may behave as if the dead person is still there and refuses to acknowledge the loss. Another way denial gets expressed is to remove all visible signs of the person's existence (e.g. clothes, photos and so on) immediately after the death; as if, by getting rid of all reminders, they will avoid dealing with the feelings.

Growing awareness

This is a very emotional part of the grieving process in that an individual can tend to be overwhelmed by strong feelings that cannot be controlled. They may experience a real yearning and urge to search for the person who has died. They may also experience a great deal of anger which may or may not be directed at other services or someone whom they perceive to have caused the death. They may also experience a great deal of despair, emptiness and depression associated with the pain of this loss. Guilt may also enter into this stage with the bereaved person feeling that he or she has neglected or harmed the dead person in some way. They can also feel extremely guilty about their own feelings and their seeming inability to get on with their life or enjoy anything any more. Anxiety may also be experienced and can develop into a real sense of panic as the full realisation of what has been lost is finally experienced.

Acceptance

For the majority of people, acceptance tends to occur approximately a year after the person has died. It is at this stage that the bereaved person is able to enter into their life experience once again and to be able to do so in the knowledge that they can be a coper and manage change without the support, love and presence of the deceased person.

Talk time

The group rules can be reinforced and students can be divided into smaller groups and focus upon the following questions:

- How would you know when a person is in any one of these stages of grief?
- What would their behaviour be like?
- What kind of support do you think they would need at each of these stages and where could they gain support or help of the right kind?

Students' responses could be recorded with one student allocated to the role of scribe. Ideas can be fed back to the group as a whole with the facilitator summarising and recording views on the flip-chart. It will also be helpful to highlight any similarities and difference in responses and to consider which kind of strategies and agencies of support would seem to be most useful at each of the grief stages.

Activity 1 – Personal grief

This activity is intended as a more personal time for reflection when students can consider a specific loss that they have encountered and how this caused them to experience grief. It will be important to consider students who have experienced major bereavement or loss and to perhaps check that they are comfortable with this activity prior to the start of the session. Students who do not wish to contribute or to participate will need to be allowed space for withdrawal from this particular aspect of the session or perhaps from the session as a whole.

Each student can be provided with the work sheet 'Personal Grief'. This asks them to consider the following questions:

- Choose one loss that you have experienced and think about the grief process.
- What was helpful or unhelpful?
- What was unhelpful?
- What did you learn about yourself and others?
- On reflection, would you have done anything different?
- How will this experience help you to deal with future loss?
- How will this experience help you to help other people deal with loss?
- Anything else?

Once students have completed this activity they may wish to discuss their experiences with others in the group and feed back to the group as a whole. However, some students may wish to keep their responses to themselves and this will need to be respected by the facilitator and group.

Activity 2 – Differences and similarities in the grief cycle

In this activity we again ask students to consider complex feelings and thoughts about death and dying. The intention is to encourage reflective discussion and for conclusions to be open-ended rather than closed.

Divide the group into small groups and give each group one of the three scenarios. Ask the students to discuss the two examples in their handout and how they are likely to be different for Kylie, her family and the school.

Ask the students to discuss the similarities and differences in the responses and grief process. Students can list key points and then feed back to the whole group.

The facilitator may need to draw out some of the key points as follows:

- It may not be helpful to ask whether it is worse if a young person dies than if an old person dies; or, similarly if a death is anticipated or sudden.
- There will be differences in how grief is experienced and there will be similarities.
- There will be perceived advantages and disadvantages to both anticipated and sudden death and students should be allowed to express these.

We would expect conclusions to be drawn along a 'more or less' continuum rather than in terms of 'either/or'.

It is not possible to predict how an individual will respond to a death.

The grief process will tend to follow the same pattern but different stages will be more or less difficult, more or less intense, and the time it takes to 'move on' will vary a lot.

Key differences in responses depend on numerous variables. Whether the death was anticipated or sudden and whether it was a young person, an old person, a person who was well known in their community or who had achieved a lot or a little and so on. Some of the many points that are likely to be made include:

Anticipated death – e.g. terminal illness

There is more opportunity for the family and school to prepare.

The school could have established links with the family. The child can be supported in school by friends and staff.

Grieving may relate to the changes caused by the illness (i.e. she didn't recognize her near the end).

The sick person may gradually withdraw and 'handover' their role within the family.

There has been a chance to complete unfinished business and to say goodbye.

Relief that they are not suffering any more.

Guilt about feeling relieved.

Sudden death – e.g. a road traffic accident

There is a sudden separation with no warning.

There may be unfinished business with no chance for the bereaved to say goodbye.

The response is reactive rather than proactive.

Feelings are likely to be more intense and more extreme.

There is no time to prepare so support may not be available immediately.

When a young person dies

A sense that this is 'before their time' and not within the natural order of things.

A desire to change places with the dead person.

Mourning for what might have been.

A feeling that it doesn't make sense and there is no comfort to be found. A questioning of religious faith.

When an adult dies

An evaluation of their life – had they achieved what they wanted?

Is it their death or our loss which we feel most?

Activity 3 – Illustrated stages

Students can be provided with the worksheet 'Draw Your Own Grief Cycle' in order to produce their own illustrated stages of grief.

Plenary

Students can reflect upon the question 'What have we learned about the stages of grief?' and the facilitator can record the students' responses and ideas on the flip-chart. It may be helpful to record the stages as headings on separate pieces of paper and to ask students to brainstorm each of the headings in turn. This activity should allow for reinforcement of the main points covered alongside identifying some of the ways in which students can help themselves and others when they are experiencing this process.

Follow-on activities

Students can write poems with the title 'Grief Doesn't Last Forever'.

Students design posters in order to illustrate the fact that crying is not a sign of weakness. It is more a sign of deep feelings which need to be expressed.

Some students may wish to produce a model for grief of their own design, e.g. depicting grief in the form of a whirlpool, a raging storm which eventually calms, an erupting volcano, etc. It may be helpful for students to share their models at the end of this activity and to explain to each other the meaning of their drawings/illustrations.

Use the Rodin sculpture *Grief* or Picasso's *Weeping Woman* as a starting point for more individual artwork.

The Grief Cycle

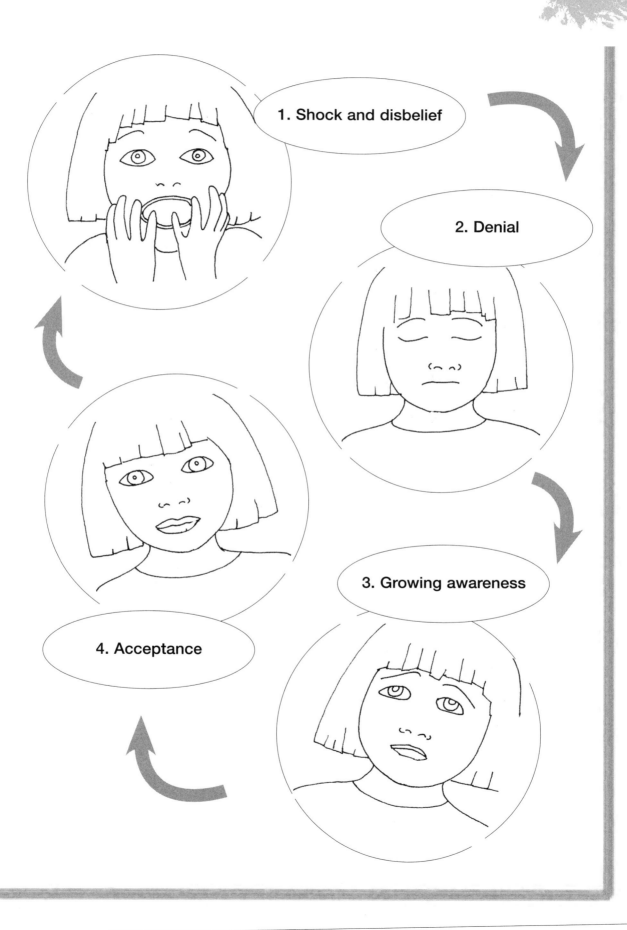

1. Shock and disbelief
2. Denial
3. Growing awareness
4. Acceptance

Personal Grief

Choose one loss that you have experienced and think about the grief process.

What was helpful?
....
....

What was unhelpful?
....
....

What did you learn?

   i) about yourself? ....
....

   ii) about others? ....
....

On reflection, would you have done anything differently?
....
....

How will this experience help you to deal with future loss?
....
....

How will this experience help you to help other people deal with loss?
....
....

Anything else?
....
....
....
....

Differences and Similarities in the Grief Cycle

Scenario one – anticipated death and sudden death

Example A – Kylie is an ordinary 14 year old girl attending her local comprehensive school. Her mum has just died after a long illness. Kylie lives at home with her dad and brother Liam.

Example B – Kylie is an ordinary 14 year old girl attending her local comprehensive school. Her mum has just died suddenly and unexpectedly. Kylie lives at home with her dad and brother Liam.

Scenario two – anticipated death and sudden death

Example C – Kylie was a 14 year old girl who has just died after a long illness. She attended her local comprehensive until recently when she became too ill to continue attending. Kylie lived at home with her brother Liam and her mum and dad.

Example D – Kylie was a 14 year old girl who has just died unexpectedly in a car accident. She attended her local comprehensive and lived at home with her brother Liam and her mum and dad.

Scenario three – a young person and an old person

Example E – Kylie is an ordinary 14 year old girl attending her local comprehensive school. Her grandmother has just died after a long illness aged 89. Kylie lives at home with her parents and her brother Liam.

Example F – Kylie is an ordinary 14 year old girl attending her local comprehensive. Her 12 year old brother Liam (who attended the same school) has just died after a long illness. Kylie lives at home with her mum and dad.

Draw Your Own Grief Cycle

This is my version of a grief cycle.

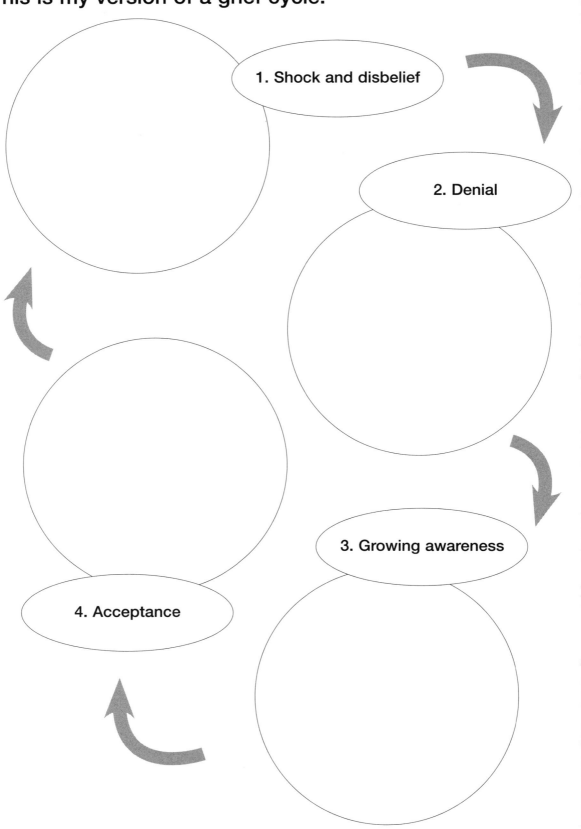

Session 10
Support and Communication

Introduction

The facilitator can introduce this session by briefly summarising the learning objectives. The students will be asked to focus on and identify ways in which they can help bereaved friends and family members. They will also be required to identify difficulties that some people have during the grieving process and in showing their grief. There will be opportunities to consider ways in which they can identify those who can help them when they are experiencing a significant loss.

Students will be given the opportunity to identify immediate resources within the community and useful organisations which can help support the bereaved. There will also be an opportunity to consider a range of strategies to relieve stress and aid relaxation.

Talk time

The group rules can be reinforced and students can then work together in groups in order to discuss and answer the following questions:

- What do we think bereaved people need most?
- What do we think bereaved people need least?

Students can record their responses on the worksheet 'Supporting Bereaved People', nominating one individual to act as scribe and another individual to feed back to the rest of the group. The facilitator may wish to summarise responses on the flip-chart pointing out any similarities and differences and highlighting the strategies that students have identified as being most useful to someone who is experiencing bereavement.

Activity 1 – What is helpful?

In this activity students are presented with a series of statements. These are recorded on statement cards found on the 'What Is Helpful?' worksheet. These can be cut out and laminated. Students are asked to consider which of the statements they would consider to be most helpful in supporting a bereaved friend. They are encouraged to discuss the statements with a partner or within the context of a smaller group and then to place the statements in rank order, i.e. which would be most helpful and which would be least helpful. The statements are as follows:

- Tell them to go to the doctor to get some anti-depressants.
- Tell them to stop worrying about things and try not to think about it.
- Don't ask them to go out for a bit in case they get too upset.
- Say that it could have been far worse than it was.
- Stay with them when you think you're needed.
- Try to make them laugh by telling them jokes.
- Talk about football or the weather.
- Give them some food and tell them to get a good night's sleep.
- Tell them they will cope eventually and get over it.
- Do some of the more mundane things or chores that they have to do for themselves.

- Encourage them to talk about their experiences and feelings.
- Tell them about your own misfortunes and how these could be much worse.
- Leave them alone.
- Give them lots of sympathy.
- Keep visiting them all the time.
- Tell them how much luckier they are than some people.
- Encourage them to cry and talk about things.
- Listen to them and don't interrupt them.
- Ignore their bereavement or loss and pretend that it didn't happen at all.
- Love them and accept them no matter how mad they might seem.

Once students have completed the activity they can feed back their ranking order to the rest of the group. The facilitator can point out any similarities or differences and encourage students to justify their ranking process.

Activity 2 – Learning to listen

Very often the shock of a death or a suicide has an enormously distressing influence on both family and friends. Those who are grieving, particularly siblings, can retreat into themselves and their isolation can make the parents, in particular, feel extremely fearful. Very often, friends are simply at a loss as to know what to say or do. This engenders feelings of helplessness and inadequacy.

However, as friends we can be there to simply listen and it is consequently important that we develop our listening skills to the greatest extent possible.

Students can be placed into groups of three designating the role of speaker, listener and observer to each participant. The speaker then talks about a real or imaginary problem that they may have. During the activity the listener can

1. Listen in silence.

2. Offer solutions non-stop.

3. Encourage the speaker to really describe his or her feelings and explore different aspects of the problem.

Afterwards, each member of the group gives their feedback as to what was the most or least helpful. The speaker feeds back first, then the listener and then the observer. Each participant should be given the opportunity to describe how they felt at each stage of the process and to identify the most and least helpful behaviours in both themselves and other participants. The exercise can be repeated with students swapping the different roles.

Students can then consider which approaches would be most useful when supporting or listening to a friend who has suffered a significant loss, either through death or suicide. They can then feed back their ideas to the group as a whole and the facilitator can highlight similarities and differences in the students' responses.

This will also be an opportunity to reinforce the key skills of good listening which may include the following:

- showing warmth and caring
- showing empathy
- giving non-judgemental acceptance
- showing respect

- being genuine
- limiting your own talking
- clarifying something when you don't understand it totally
- summarise throughout to make sure that you have got it right
- asking open-ended questions
- not interrupting
- listening out for the feelings that the person's displaying or showing underneath what they are saying
- not jumping to conclusions or making assumptions
- trying to listen for overtones
- really concentrating and being attentive.

Activity 3 – Top ten tips for supporting someone who is grieving

The facilitator can ask the students to focus on the following question:

How would I support a grieving friend?

Ideas can be recorded by the facilitator on the flip-chart and the students can be given the opportunity to feed back to the group as a whole. Key skills, qualities and strategies can be identified by the students and facilitator working together. Students then can make up their own top ten tips and design posters to illustrate these.

Plenary

The facilitator can ask students to focus upon the following questions:

- What have we learnt in today's session?
- What do we consider to be the best ways to help and support people who are bereaved?

The facilitator can encourage students to contribute their responses recording these on the flip-chart. Summarise the best strategies in terms of supporting and helping each other through the process of grieving with a particular focus on the importance of learning to be an effective listener.

Follow-on activities

Circle of support

The students are each provided with the 'Circle of Support' worksheet, which they can complete on an individual basis or with the support of peers as appropriate. This activity asks students to identify someone who is a very close friend who can support them throughout the process of loss and grieving. They are also asked to identify someone within the home context and outside of the home context who also will be able to support them throughout this process. They are then asked to identify the ways in which these people would be able to support them through the following actions:

- Not betraying my confidence.
- Not making me have to pretend when I am with them.
- Not trying to cheer me up all of the time.
- Not ignoring my loss and pretending that it actually hasn't happened to me.
- To be with me and stay with me when I actually need them.

- To give me a real hug and allow me to cry.
- Not to tell me just to go and get anti-depressants from my doctor.
- Not to tell me that it could have been much worse than it actually is.
- Listening to me and not getting bored with me going on and on.

The students can discuss ways of coping with stress. It may be helpful to highlight strategies covered in *Strictly Stress* (Rae, 2001) to then consider which stress management strategies may be helpful for someone who is bereaved or experiencing a significant loss.

Relaxation script

Provide the students with a copy of the 'Relaxation Script', which they may wish to practise. They can also consider the way in which such a technique may support someone who is experiencing a significant bereavement or loss.

Students can investigate the range of resources in the community and useful organisations which may be helpful in terms of supporting the bereaved. A display can then be made which includes all of this information for future reference and perhaps presented in the form of a useful booklet for other students in the school to pick up and use as and when appropriate. Students can decide which agencies they wish to include and these may be reflective of the range of cultures/religious/ ethnic backgrounds within the group. Groups included may include the Lesbian and Gay Bereavement Project, National HIV Prevention Service, Samaritans, SANDS, The Compassionate Friends, Foundation for Black Bereaved Families, Jewish Bereavement Counselling Service, Relate, Age Concern, Libraries, Community Health Council, Community Relations Council, Social Services, etc.

Supporting Bereaved People

S10

What do we think bereaved people need most?

....
....
....
....
....
....
....
....
....

What do we think bereaved people need least?

....
....
....
....
....
....
....
....
....

What is Helpful?

- Tell them to go to the doctor to get some anti-depressants.
- Tell them to stop worrying about things and try not to think about it.
- Don't ask them to go out for a bit in case they get too upset.
- Say that it could have been far worse than it was.
- Stay with them when you think you're needed.
- Try to make them laugh by telling them jokes.
- Talk about football or the weather.
- Give them some food and tell them to get a good night's sleep.
- Tell them they will cope eventually and get over it.
- Do some of the more mundane things or chores that they have to do for themselves.
- Encourage them to talk about their experiences and feelings.
- Tell them about your own misfortunes and how these could be much worse.
- Leave them alone.
- Give them lots of sympathy.
- Keep visiting them all the time.
- Tell them how much luckier they are than some people.
- Encourage them to cry and talk about things.
- Listen to them and don't interrupt them.
- Ignore their bereavement or loss and pretend that it didn't happen at all.
- Love them and accept them no matter how mad they might seem.

These statements can be copied onto A4 cards and laminated.

Circle of Support

Someone outside of the home

Someone at home

A close friend

How can each person help?

....
....
....
....
....

Relaxation Script

Prepare

You'll need to be in a quiet room with no distractions. Sit in a chair with both feet planted firmly on the ground and legs uncrossed. Put you hands in your lap, close your eyes and off you go!

Clench your fists – hold them, feel the tension, then let your fingers loose and relax. Feel yourself relax all over. Then repeat.

Bend from your elbows and tense up your biceps. Feel the tension, then put your arms out and let them relax. Repeat. Really feel the tension and the relaxation in your muscles.

Straighten up your arms so that you feel the tension in the upper parts – within the muscles on the backs of you arms. Then let your arms hang loose and feel the tension disappear. Repeat.

Close your eyes extremely tightly. Feel the tension in your eyelids and around your eye sockets. Then relax your eyes – still keeping them closed and enjoy the sensation. Repeat.

Frown and pull the muscles in your forehead together. Then relax and feel your forehead becoming smooth and relaxed. Repeat.

Clench your fists tightly. Relax and open your lips a little. Repeat.

Close your lips together tightly. Then relax and focus on the difference between the relaxed position and the tensed position. Feel yourself relax all over your face, in your mouth and in your throat. Repeat.

Lift your head up and let it drop back as far as you can (without any straining). Feel the tension in your neck. Move your head from left to right and right to left, feeling the tension moving into each side of your neck. Next lift your head forwards and press your chin downwards against your chest. Then return your head to an upright position and relax. Repeat.

Lift your shoulders up and hold in the tension then drop and relax. Feel this relaxation spreading to your back and all the parts of your face and neck. Repeat.

Concentrate on relaxing your whole body and breathe slowly in and out. Each time you exhale imagine all the tension leaving your body. Next breathe in, inhale deeply and hold your breath. Then breathe out feeling your chest relax. Breathe in deeply through your nose counting slowly to five. Then exhale slowly, letting your breath free to the count of five. Repeat.

Relaxation Script (cont.)

Next, tighten up your stomach muscles. Hold your stomach in as tightly as you can and then let the muscles relax. Concentrate on the two different sensations of tension and relaxation. Next push your stomach out and hold in this position prior to relaxing the muscles again. Repeat.

Tighten up your thighs and buttocks and then release and relax. Press down on your heels and then relax. Repeat.

Press your feet into the floor and feel your calf-muscles tensing. Release and relax. Repeat.

Bend up your ankles towards your body and hold them tightly. Relax and release them. Repeat.

Finally, let yourself relax all over – from your toes, through your feet, ankles, calves, shins, knees, thighs, hips, stomach and lower back. Feel the tension escape. Relax your upper back, chest, shoulders, arms and fingers. Feel your neck, jaws and facial muscles relax. Breathe in deeply and then slowly let your breath out. Count slowly from 1-10 and then open your eyes.

You are now truly relaxed.

Session 11
Remembering and Celebrating

Introduction

The facilitator can remind students of the work completed in Session 6 and particularly enforce the ground rule to respect different beliefs and cultural practices.

A main aim of this session is to introduce the topic of funerals and to discuss what actually has to be organised once someone has died. Customs and outward forms of observance and celebration vary greatly from place to place and this session will give students an opportunity to consider the wide variety of ways in which people construct this framework in order to express their grief and sorrow. A funeral service generally gives a structure which enables the disposal of the body. It also publicly confirms the death for the community itself whilst symbolising the change in status of those in the family.

This session also highlights the importance of remembering and celebrating the lives of those who have died through formal services and more personal, informal means.

Talk time

Separate the students into groups and focus on the following questions:

- Why do we have funerals?
- What customs do we know about that surrounds these?
- How might these customs and celebrations help people who are bereaved?
- What feelings do we associate with saying goodbye in this way?

It will be important to emphasise the need for all students to contribute their ideas, particularly regarding customs from within their own community. One student per group can record the ideas and these can then be fed back to the group as a whole with the facilitator summarising the main points and highlighting significant similarities and any differences.

Activity 1 – Celebrating lives

This activity is aimed at promoting a positive attitude towards moving forwards and celebrating and remembering those whom we have loved. Celebrating someone's life can be done throughout the grieving process and is something that is generally ongoing in terms of both remembering and appreciating the individual concerned.

Students are presented with the worksheet 'Celebrating Lives' in which they can brainstorm as many different ways as possible that they might wish to remember or celebrate someone's life. It may be helpful to have a short brainstorming session on this prior to asking students to complete the task so that they can share ideas and strategies. Ideas may include the following:

- making up memory books
- designing and making up special photograph albums
- writing cards
- making a tape
- creating a memory poster of a special day
- making up a tape of special music that the person loved
- making a memento box in which there are lots of trinkets or special things that the person loved or owned.

Activity 2 – Celebration shields

Students can be provided with the worksheet 'Celebration Shields'. Ask them to design their own shields which can be divided up into four main sections as follows:

1. An illustration of the student's past life.
2. An illustration or brief description of how they would see their own future.
3. An illustration or brief description of people who are closest to the student.
4. An illustration or brief description of how they see or perceive death.

Students may also wish to formulate their own mottos and these can be written underneath the celebratory shield. The facilitator can ask students to feed back on this activity and compare ideas, perceptions and future dreams.

Activity 3 – Saying goodbye

Either work from a newspaper report of a real event or devise a scenario that might be familiar and of relevance and interest to the students.

The focus in this activity will be on deaths which are possibly violent and unexpected. This activity is culturally sensitive and the facilitator should take account of the views and experiences of the student group.

The students are asked to imagine that they are directly involved in the event and face death in a few minutes.

The facilitator can ask:

- Who would you choose to send a last text message to say goodbye?
- What would you write in your final text message?

Plenary

Students can address the question: 'What have we learned about funerals, saying goodbye and the processes involved in celebrating the lives of those who have died?' The facilitator can support students by summarising the main points covered within the session whilst also emphasising the differences and similarities in customs celebrating death.

Follow-on activities

It may be useful to invite a speaker from the British Humanist Association to the group in order to hear how they would plan their own funeral service and their reasons for adopting this form of service.

Irish families often have a wake before the funeral when many people from the local community will mourn the death of their friend or colleague. Very often these become quite celebratory affairs. Students can decide upon how they would like to celebrate a friend's life or a family member's life or even their own lives by designing their own wake and considering the kinds of music they would like to have played, the food they would like to have served, the drinks they would like to have served, etc.

Public figures generally tend to have an obituary published in the newspapers and in order to introduce this particular activity the facilitator may wish to provide the students with some examples of these. These can be read out prior to asking the students to then either write their own obituary entitled 'A Tribute to Me' or to write an obituary for someone who they know that has died. The students can initially think about the sorts of things they would like to be remembered for and can then begin to summarise the main points of their life that they think are of most significance. Volunteers can then be asked to share these with the whole group and the facilitator can identify some of the common features of these tributes/epitaphs. The main feature will obviously be that these speeches or descriptions will tend to focus on what was good about the particular person and the things that were positive that they have achieved in their lives. If students wish, they can obviously make humorous epitaphs or eulogies and this will, to some extent, defuse some of the more uncomfortable feelings which may occur around this particular activity.

Celebrating Lives

S11

How would you remember and celebrate someone's life?

Record your ideas here.

Celebration Shields

Design your own celebration shield.

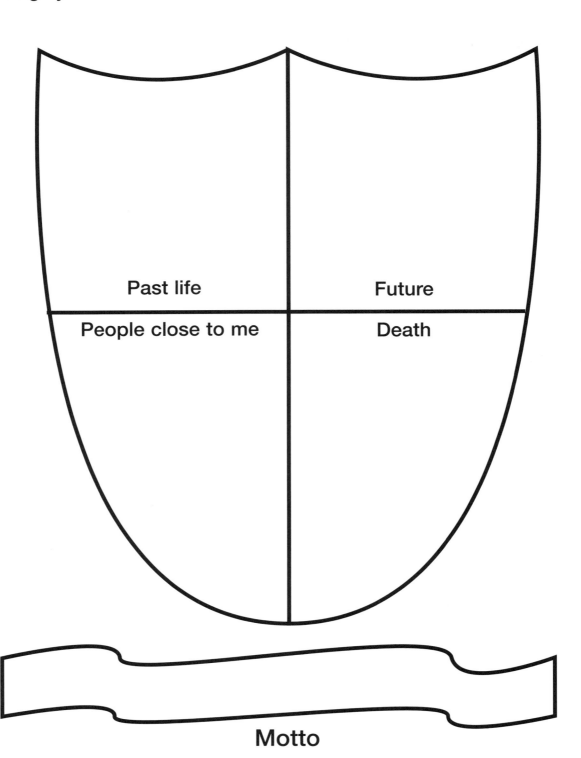

| Past life | Future |
| People close to me | Death |

Motto

Saying Goodbye

Imagine you have only five minutes left to live.

Who would you choose to send a last text message to say goodbye?

What would you write in your final text message?

Fill in the phone screen below.

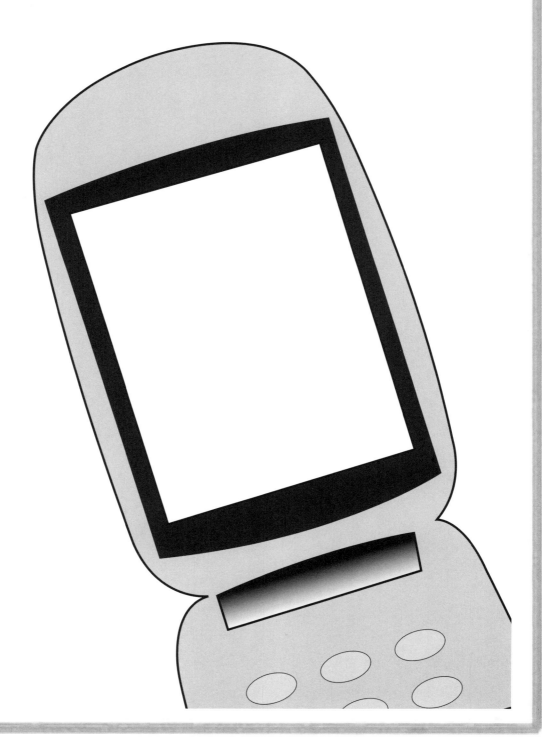

Session 12
Review

Introduction

In this last session the students are invited to review the programme. This final session also provides the facilitator with an opportunity to model how to make endings meaningful, thus providing the necessary sense of closure for the group as a whole.

Talk time

The facilitator can remind the students that this is the last session and that part of the session will focus on ending things and saying goodbye.

The facilitator can write the numbers one to eleven on a flip-chart and then ask the students to try to remember each session and what topics were covered.

Activity 1 – Individual review

The students can be asked to complete the worksheet 'My Review of the Programme'. This framework encourages them to identify:

- Things I liked.
- Things I didn't like.
- Something I would change.
- Something new I learned.

It may then be helpful to encourage students to share their responses with a friend or via a circle discussion with the group as a whole.

Activity 2 – Where do you stand?

This activity reinforces some of the learning that has taken place in the programme. It also allows the facilitator to assess whether he has achieved the objectives of educating students about the facts of death, loss and grief, promoting tolerance and of developing students' emotional literacy.

When you evaluate the programme it may be helpful to refer to what happens in this activity as a way of seeing tangible outcomes. We would hope that by now students would have moved some way towards meeting some of the key aims of the programme as outlined in Aims (p10):

- To develop emotional literacy (that is, to recognise, understand, manage and express emotions in ourselves and others).
- To encourage students to become more aware of the links between feelings thinking and behaviour.
- To further develop their ability to reflect, joint problem-solve and work with others.
- To develop empathy.
- To increase self-esteem.
- To develop confidence in dealing with difficult situations.
- To improve students' social and group work skills.

- To develop communication and relationship skills.
- To promote resilience, to help students identify and gain a deeper understanding of the feelings associated with loss, separation and bereavement.
- To promote respect and tolerance.
- To understand the grieving process and the ways in which people can be helped through this process.
- To understand and value the afterlife beliefs, death rituals and funeral customs of other cultures and religions.

The tables will need to be moved for this activity and the group rules can be restated if needed. Ask the students to stand in different ends of the room depending on how strongly they feel about the statement you make. If appropriate, make up some statements to suit the particular requirements of your group and practise with a few 'low risk' statements such as:

- You should always clean your teeth before you go to bed.
- People should recycle all their waste paper and glass.

Students can be asked to position themselves at each end of the room, for example, left if you agree strongly with the statement and right if you disagree strongly and somewhere in the middle if you are more ambivalent. When the students have moved into position you could ask individuals to say something about why they are standing where they are. The following statements can be read out by the facilitator as appropriate:

- We should not talk about death because it's embarrassing for everyone.
- There is no such thing as a perfect family.
- Pupils who get excluded should always be given another chance.
- Suicide is wrong.
- People should be allowed to have their death assisted if they choose.
- Women should be able to have an abortion on demand.
- The most common cause of death amongst teenagers is road accidents.
- Most religions have more things in common than differences.
- Children should not be allowed to go to funerals.
- Everyone grieves in their own way. Whatever way you do it is OK.
- I would be able to support a friend who was bereaved.
- I don't care what happens to my body after I die.
- I would like to live to 100.
- Children who get into trouble at school are often in trouble at home too.
- You can tell how someone is feeling just by looking at them.
- Refugees in this country have probably lost more than they will ever gain.
- I would go to the funeral of anyone who died from this school.
- I know why people of some religions wear white to funerals and others wear black.
- People grieve differently and individually.
- Grieving allows us to come to terms with loss.
- I think I will be able to deal with bereavement better now I've done this course.
- I would know what I'd do if someone in this class was bereaved.
- Even if someone who has been bereaved looks OK you know they must be grieving.

- I know what I'll do if someone in this class's mum and dad split up.
- It's important to understand that refugees and asylum seekers have had a hard time.
- Children should be allowed to go to funerals.
- I respect the religious beliefs of other people in this class.
- People who have been bereaved need to get drunk so they can forget about it.
- I believe in life after death/I believe in reincarnation.
- I would be cremated, not buried, when I die.
- If someone commits suicide they will go to hell.

Activity 3 – Circle

In this activity, the facilitator can ask the students to take part in a circle using the 'finish the sentence' activity, completing the following sentences:

- Something I know about you that I didn't know before is....
- Something you said that I remember is....
- Something I liked is....
- Something I found difficult is...

This activity, to some extent, mirrors the individual reviews conducted at the start of the session and should, therefore, feel reasonably comfortable for the students involved.

Plenary

In this final plenary the students will be provided with the opportunity to reflect on the things that they have learnt during the entire course. It will be helpful to focus upon the following questions:

- What do we think we have learnt about the grieving process?
- To what extent do we think these sessions will help us in the future should we suffer bereavement?
- To what extent do we feel better equipped to help others who are bereaved?
- Have we increased our understanding of others cultures or belief systems in this area?
- What kind and type of support is available to us and others in terms of coping more effectively with bereavement?
- What was the most useful session and why?
- What was the least useful session and why?
- Which aspects of the session were the most enjoyable or the most profitable, e.g. talking time, brainstorming activities, plenaries, role-plays, etc?
- If you were running this course how would you change it to make it better for next time?

Follow-on activities

Students may wish to design an outline for their own course on grief and the management of bereavement.

Students may wish to investigate how grief and loss affects much younger children than themselves and to construct some activities for younger children in order to support them through the grieving process.

My Review of the Programme

What do you think about what we did?

Finish the sentence:

The activities I liked most were ....

....

The activities I liked least were ....

....

The session I learned most in was...

....

The session I learned least in was ....

....

Something I would change if I was teaching this course ....

....

Something I know now that I didn't know before ....

....

Someone in this class who I feel like I know better now is........................

....

Something I'd like to find out more about ....

....

Something I'd like to do some more work on is ....

....

Anything else: ....

....

....

....

References

Best, C. & Mead, C. (1996) Trauma in school: The Psychology of helping in A. Sigston, P.Curran, A.Labram and S.Wolfendale (1996) *Psychology in Practice with Young People, Families and Schools.* David Fulton Publishers.

Black, D. (1978) The Bereaved Child. *Journal of Clinical Psychology & Psychiatry,* 19, 287-292.

Black, D. (1998) Bereavement in Childhood. *British Medical Journal,* Vol. 316.

Bowlby, J. (1979) *The Making and Breaking of Affectional Bonds.* London: Tavistock.

Brown, E. (1999) *Loss, Change and Grief: An Educational Perspective.* David Fulton Publishers.

Christian, L.G. (1997) Children and Death. *Young Children,* 52,4, 76-80.

Durkin, C. (2000) Transition: the child's perspective. *Educational and Child Psychology,* Vol 17 (1)

Farrell, P. (1999) The Limitations of Current Theories in Understanding Bereavement and Grief. *Counselling,* May 1999.

Dyregrov, A. (1990) *Grief in Children: A Handbook for Adults.* London: Jessica Kingsley Publishers.

Lindsay, B. & Elsegood, J. (Eds) (1996) *Working with children in Grief and Loss.* Bailiere Tindall.

Pankhurst, L. (1998) Coping with divorce and separation. *Co-ordinate,* March 1998

Park, J. (1999) (Director of Antidote: The Campaign for Emotional Literacy) unpublished paper presented at South of England Psychology Services Conference December 1999.

Pennells, M. & Smith, S.C. (1995) *The Forgotten Mourners.* London: Jessica Kingsley Publishers.

Pettle, S.A. & Britten, C.M. (1995) Talking with children about death and dying. *Child: care, health and development,* 21,6,387-394.

Plant, S. and Stoate, P. (1989) *Loss and Change: Resources for use in a personal and social education programme.* Southgate Publishers.

Plath, S. (1981) *The Collected Poems.* Harper Row.

Rae, T. (2004) *Emotional Survival: An Emotional Literacy Course for High School Students.* Bristol: Lucky Duck Publishing.

Reid, J. (1995) Dealing with Divorce. *Nursery Work,* July 1995.

Ribbens McCarthy J. with Jessop J. (2005) *Young People, Bereavement and Loss Disruptive Transitions.* National Childrens Bureau / Joseph Rowntree Foundation.

Rogers, B. & Pryor, J. (1998) *Divorce and separation: the Outcomes for Children.* Report completed by the Joseph Rowntree Foundation (IABN 1 85935 043 7).

Salzberger-Wittenberg, I., Henry, G. and Osborne, E. (1983) *The Emotional Experience of Learning and Teaching.* Routledge.

Sharp, P. (2001) *Nurturing Emotional Literacy: A Practical Guide for Parents and those in the Caring Professions.* London: David Fulton Publishers.

Sunderland M.2003 Tripp, J.H. & Crockett, M. (1996) The Exeter Family Study. *Family Law,* Vol. 26.

Ward, B & Associates (1993) *Good Grief Exploring Feelings, Loss and Death with Over Elevens and Adults. A Holistic Approach.* London: Jessica Kingsley Publishers.

Warner, R. (1992) Loss and grief in the lives of newly arrived bilingual pupils. *Multicultural Teaching,* 10 (2).

Webster, A. (1995) Family Breakdowns. *Child Education,* June 1995.

Wells, R. (1998) *Helping Children Cope with Grief.* London: Sheldon Press.